Vital Signs, Scorecards, and Goals

The Power of Meaningful Measurement

by Kevin McManus

Great Systems!

www.greatsystems.com

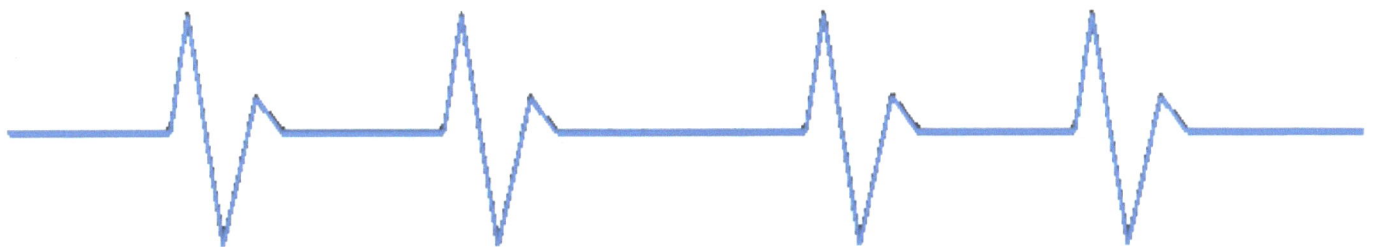

**Additional information on workshops and other materials related
to this workbook can be obtained by contacting**

Kevin McManus
Great Systems!
(206) 226-8913
E-Mail: kevin@greatsystems.com
www.greatsystems.com

Other books and workbooks by the author include:

Are You Ready for 21st Century Leadership?
You Can't Win Indy in an Edsel - How to Develop a High Performance Work Culture
Are Your Teams Working? - Keys to Team Effectiveness
Supervising for High Performance
The Fundamentals of Lean Tools and Concepts
Avoiding Extinction: How to Add Personal Value in a Changing Workplace
Unleash the Power of Project Teams

Vital Signs, Scorecards, and Goals
The Power of Meaningful Measurement

Table of Contents

Chapters

Individual and Group Exercises

The Genesis of This Book

This book began back in 1997 as a workbook that described how to implement balanced scorecards on the front lines in an organization. It was one of the first workbooks I wrote and self-published, and I wrote it primarily to help teach others how to use the tools that I had created and helped others install as Production Manager for a candy company. I had yet to realize the true power of the tools themselves – this power came to light as I found better ways to design and use each tool, first as and Director of Quality in a trucking company and then as a plant manager for a flavored syrup manufacturer.

That was near twenty years ago. Today, balanced scorecards, key performance indicators, and 'stoplight' color coding of results are ubiquitous in business – almost all large organizations use them in one form or another. In fact, we have gone past the point of full tool use when it comes to coloring our scorecards and are fast entering the world of tool miss-use. Too many people are getting colored 'Red' too often when measures they have little effect over bounce into the 'bad zone'. I am also seeing more and more organizations, even the good ones, struggling with (1) effectively using their data and (2) moving closer to sustained process excellence.

As you might suspect, other changes happened as well over the past twenty years. From a measurement work system perspective, I continued to get unwanted validation from my customers that the wrong measures were being used to measure the wrong things, for the wrong reasons.

More importantly, I gained something positive. I had to have it pointed out to me, and the person who pointed it out did not know they were doing so at the time, but that is how serendipity works. Yes, there is a place for serendipity in a measurement book. My learning was simple – we fail all too often to measure at the process level. The more I looked into this problem, the more widespread I found it to be.

I had been using this approach to measurement for years, and I took it for granted that other process owners did the same. I had failed to see the drift in measure focus from the front lines to the site, business unit, or corporation level that was occurring. I had assumed that all process owners tracked their daily process errors just like I did, and used their data to see if their error correction strategies were working or not. I did not realize that people were getting lost trying to explain why the big numbers were going up and down, instead of just up as requested, because the measures in use were losing their sensitivity as time progressed.

In summary, I am writing this book to address measurement problems that are cultural in nature by sharing practices that have worked for others, including myself. We can choose to use better measures (more leading ratios), use them more effectively (make better decisions), and regularly capture and use the right mix of process level measures (vital signs). It is my hope that by laying out some sound logic and easy-to-use examples, I can help you improve your measurement systems and the processes they are intended to support.

For reference, you might want to also check out some of the other books I have written to assist you with your team or organizational improvement efforts. These books and workbooks will provide you with additional information and examples of other process and work system improvement tools.

Keep improving!

Potential Learning Opportunities

Building a Better Measurement System

- How to select those measures that best reflect process health

- How to build scorecards that give an accurate snapshot of key process outcome performance

- How to set challenging, but realistic, goals that are linked to both strategies and the daily job

- How to develop plans for consistent measurement system use and improvement over time

What are your goals for reading this book?

Many articles and books have been written over the last twenty-five or so years, most notably those by Kaplan and Norton, touting the competitive and strategic benefits of implementing the balanced scorecard concept. Most of these publications focused more on using this technique at the "top" of an organization, and became widely accepted, as key performance indicators were defined and red-yellow-green goals were set by organizations of all types. Fewer documents addressed what it would take to implement this tool on the front lines – at the process level - and have it effectively used on a daily basis by each work team member across a site, business unit, or organization. The goal of this book is to provide a daily, process-based focus.

This book describes the steps that have been taken in both service and manufacturing companies to implement this concept at the work team, or front line, level. This process is simple, and yet, effective. Its use results in work teams that are focused on how they can impact the goals of the company and understand how their work systems and daily efforts can be directed towards changes that really make a difference.

By reading this book, participating in the workshop, and/or experimenting with one or more of the tools in your organization, you can expect to accomplish the following:

- Learn about the basics of effective measure selection and analysis as they apply to work teams, and organizational effectiveness in general.
- Gain an overview of a simple approach to daily process measurement that works.
- Identify steps that your organization or work group could take to make your processes for capturing, crunching, and analyzing data more effective.

This book describes why better measures are necessary and the types of impact using great measures effectively can have. It also looks at the benefits that can be realized by making meaningful measurement system improvements. Focus will be placed on how vital signs and scorecards are created for, and used by, process teams, and the steps that are required to make process measurement a living part of any organization. Most importantly, the book contains examples of the basic tools required to measure more effectively.

Great Systems!
"Simple systems, great results!"

Navigating This Book

Design It
- The Case for Meaningful Measurement
- Building Codes, Design Options and Outcomes Ranking

Build It
- Selecting Process Counts and Ratios
- Building Balanced Scorecards at all Levels

Use It
- How the Best Review Performance and Set Goals
- Options for Recognizing High Performance

Improve It
- Best Practice Approaches for Measuring Work Systems
- Planning for Measurement System Improvement

Design It – If the design is flawed, we cannot expect the system it is based on to work right. As with building a house or simply paving a new patio, building codes exist to help ensure building integrity. The concept is the same for work systems, but we seem to fail to make this connection, and such codes have not formally been defined. Perhaps our measurement systems are often flawed because we usually don't have blueprints for building a better measurement system. Building something without a blueprint is risky however, and the risk of structural failure is high.

Build It – Building a high performance work system is essentially the same as building a high performance car, body, or home. The tools we use, and the parts required, are different, but the process of creating a design, and turning it into something for people to use, is conceptually the same. In turn, there are better tools than others for measuring process performance, just as there are relatively more effective ways to set goals, analyze data, and trend process behavior over time. *One goal of this book is to provide you with some great measurement system blueprints to use – blueprints that are based on systems used by some of the best companies.*

Use It – One of the things that even high performing companies struggle with is effectively USING the variety of data they have at their disposal. It is a result of such struggles, and other factors, that terms like big data, informatics, and data analytics have come into vogue. These concepts, and the tools that facilitate their use, are intended to help us make better use of the myriad of information we have available. One might argue that if we were using the right measures, we would not have to use so many to create a picture of how we are doing, and we would not get lost so easily. Think vital signs … think about how vital signs are used to diagnose and treat problems.

Improve It – Best practice organizations review key work system designs against the set of results produced by those designs at least yearly, looking for ways to further improve a measure's sensitivity, accuracy, and usefulness. With information that is publically available, it is relatively easy to create a system redesign roadmap for most work systems, including measurement systems. At a minimum, measurement systems can be improved yearly by improving the mix of selected measures, identifying more relevant and new benchmarks, and streamlining data capture and crunch processes.

The Case for Meaningful Measurement

The Hammer

- What common measurement system design mistakes are made?

- What design flaws or usage errors might exist in your own measurement system?

- What best practices exist as possible system enhancements?

OR

Are your measures used to predict future success?

What common measurement system design mistakes are made?

I wrote this book because I wanted people to stop making the same silly measurement mistakes, with one big mistake being the excessive use of lagging indicators in the key performance indicator (KPI) mix. Worse yet, we seem to also be obsessed with using high level counts, as opposed to process-based ratios, when it comes to gauging the performance of a given area, person, or team and making key, often big dollar, decisions.

To what degree do you use your measures to predict future success?

When I ask this question to a group, I typically get blank stares as a response. To most, measures and prediction go together usually on the weekends, and beer and sports are also often involved. Most organizations fail to use their measures as indicators of future performance, as evidenced by the limited use of control limits on charts and the even more limited use of the term 'sigma' in everyday conversation to help explain the weather.

What best practices exist as possible system enhancements?

This book includes examples of 'best practice' measurement types, scorecard designs, data capture techniques, and implementation steps. There are a lot of possibilities to consider in the measurement system big picture, just as it is easy to get lost in the weeds debating whether or not something can be accurately measured or not. I have found it works best if you start with the basics - start by defining the vital signs for the key processes you own.

What performance gaps might exist in your own measurement system?

As you read through this book, consider making comparisons between the measurement systems and tools described here and those you are familiar with. Addressing system design flaws, such as lagging indicator overreliance and excessive count use, can help you gain better insights into (1) the factors that influence process performance and (2) the types of change needed to shift process outcomes over time.

Great Systems!
"Simple systems, great results!"

Why Measure?

Why Should You Measure?

- To catch people doing something wrong
- To hold people accountable
- To provide a focus
- To improve systems

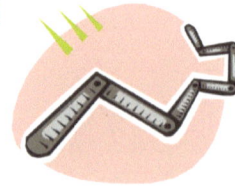

Assumptions that Emerge

- I guess we can't be trusted
- We can't, or won't, hold ourselves accountable
- We don't need data to find or make improvements
- We don't have time for proactive process stuff

When people are pressured ...

- They can work to improve the work system or process
- They can distort the system
- They can distort the data

Source: "Understanding Variation – The Key to Managing Chaos"
D. Wheeler, SPC Press, 1993

Most people measure for the wrong reasons – they use measures in an attempt to control, or at least keep track of, people. Of course, people figure this out. They also soon learn how to dodge the system by distorting the numbers, or the system itself, to keep the 'pain' to a minimum.

Measures SHOULD be used to monitor system performance (keep it between the lines) and predict future system performance (what are the odds of a goal being achieved). Step change shifts in our trends should indicate when innovations are gaining traction. Measures should also help us make wiser resource investment decisions by giving us feedback on the performance of past investments. **Measuring is all about looking for fact-based patterns and relationships**.

Fact-based feedback affects human behavior, and in turn, performance. Also, without reliable and consistent fact-based feedback, how do we know where to invest our limited resources? How will we really know if our investments are paying off? How will we know if our processes are performing as expected, let alone improving?

Imagine This Challenge ...

You have to control the temperature of someone else's shower ...

But you can't talk to them, hear them, or feel the water!

Why do you need to measure?

Why Trend Lines Really Matter

- Trend lines are needed to observe process behavior over time
- Trend lines show you the rate of change a system is experiencing
- Process variation cannot be understood without trend lines
- Trend analysis helps you find and fix problems faster
- Multiple trend lines allow you to do correlation and gap analysis
- Trend analysis helps build sound theories about the factors driving performance
- Trend analysis helps you prove that your fixes worked

Why is a picture worth a thousand words?

When I was working as an Industrial Engineer early in my career, I did not think about measurement systems very much, if at all. From my perspective, efficiency (performance to standard) and cost were the two most important things. After all, that was where most of the time, energy, and emotion seemed to be being spent by those who worked around me. I saw trend lines being used to an even lesser degree at my first two employers.

My perception of measurement changed drastically after learning from Peter Senge that the Sanskrit roots of the terms "measure" and "illusion" were the same. As an engineer, I had been taught that measures were absolutes, always required, and usually believed. As I progressed in my career, I discovered that we tend to measure things that we are uncertain about - if we think we know how something works or performs, we see no need to measure it. The mistake we make however is in thinking we understand a given work system when we don't. We are not measuring certain things because we don't think we need to.

It is one battle to get people to use certain measures – to convince them that something even needs to be measured at all. It is perhaps a greater challenge to get them to <u>effectively</u> trend the collected data over time. Process behavior lines – trend lines – are the foundation for theory development, followed by learning and improvement. At least that is how it is supposed to work.

More often than not, we don't have the data in a form that allows it to be trended. It may be scattered across several daily reports, for example. If we do have all the data in one place, we most likely don't have any type of control limits on the charts that are based on such data. Pie chart use tends to significantly outrank line chart use in the non-financial arena. Remember, trend lines are the foundation for theory building, for creating questions like "What is causing the process to behave that way?" or "How will we know if our changes are working or not?".

Most importantly, process variation cannot be understood without trend lines and control limits, and if we don't understand process variation, we can't predict future process performance with any accuracy. Failing to explore process variation through trending-based questions might also cause us to miss chances to improve measure sensitivity (better collection or calculation methods) or find and fix common cause process errors.

Great Systems!
"Simple systems, great results!"

Exploring Measurement System Maturity

Daily Report Reviews

Trend Lines

Control Charts

No Measurement

Month Vs. Month Comparisons

Link to Actions

Meaningful Measurement

Most organizations fall on this end

Improvement occurs faster over here

Process teams may fall at different places on the spectrum

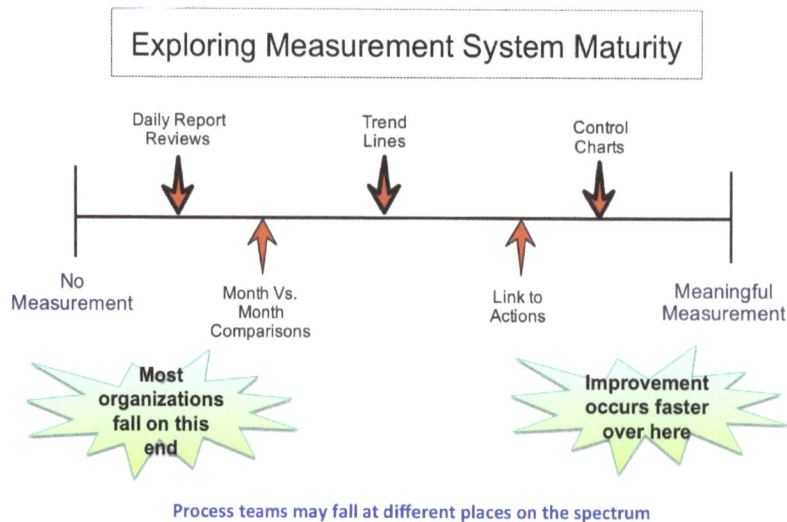

We tend to measure for the wrong reasons. We measure to trap people, to hold them accountable, or to prove that they were 'doing something wrong.' Rarely do we measure to understand systems and our choices better, which are really the primary reasons for measuring. We cannot know everything about what makes a system work, but we can use measurement to help us understand systems better.

There are really only four types of real measures, with all of them being some form of ratio. Time ratios and cost ratios are used the most often. Percentage ratios are used to measure some form of relationship as well. Ratios that show how one variable performs against another (i.e. miles per gallon) are perhaps the most powerful, but we tend to use this type of ratio less - because we are not pursuing systems understanding as our measurement goal.

Operational definitions and measurement procedures are also key, and often lacking. Without these sets of standard definitions and practices, people can measure what they want and make it look like they are giving you what you want. Even without the intent to deceive (protect oneself), a lack of operational definitions leads to confusion about what should be counted, what should be ignored, and how the data should be 'crunched.' For example, Goggle 'hanging chad'.

Measures mean little when they are not part of a trend line - they are only snapshots. One key to systems understanding is to look at a system's performance (behavior) over time and build theories based on what the picture shows us. The graph, or picture, is the starting point of systems improvement, not the end result that is desired. Similarly, analyzing trends means little if you do not do so with a diverse group of stakeholders and an open mind towards learning.

Measuring correctly teaches us about what our processes and systems are capable of. In other words, great trend analysis shows us what type of results we can expect from our systems - if we want a level of performance that is outside the current capability of the system, fundamental systems changes must be made to reach that higher level of performance.

When we set performance goals that are outside of our current system performance range, we should also know what system changes are expected to help us get there. Simply 'asking', or even paying, for higher levels of performance might work for a short amount of time, but these strategies become very difficult to sustain over the long term.

6

A Quick Needs Assessment

On a scale from 1 (rarely) to 5 (almost all of the time), rate your need for using a balanced scorecard process:

	Rarely		Almost Always		
We tend to focus on one type of measure at the expense of others	1	2	3	4	5
Our workgroups tend to focus mainly on their own success	1	2	3	4	5
Most of our employees are not aware of company costs	1	2	3	4	5
Service suffers at times because of a 'bottom line' focus	1	2	3	4	5
Rules are broken to make certain measures improve	1	2	3	4	5

TOTAL SCORE

The LOWER your score, the more BALANCED you are!

You can use the above assessment to get a quick look at the relative strengths and weaknesses of your current measurement system design. *The goal is to have a low score, as in golf.* Even though I first created this survey for use with balanced scorecard implementation over 15 years ago, most of the mistakes the survey highlights are still being made, even though scorecards are now in use, across most organizations.

We use the wrong measures – Having a high percentage of leading ratios in your measure mix should be the goal here. The tendency is to focus on measuring things that are relatively easier to measure or count, like work hours, headcount, costs, and units produced or served. We also tend to focus on higher level, aggregate measures, instead of process-based measures. This practice introduces variation into the chart that does not really exist, and can actually hide problem areas over time as the higher level of variation is accepted as the norm.

We don't analyze the data right – Our biggest error here is the practice of comparing monthly counts – usually dollars – to each other as a performance review technique. Also, the absence of process-level data makes it tough to troubleshoot problems, so we usually fall back on debating why a given number is going up or down, or is worse than expected. How often do our expectations exceed the capability of the process however?

We put weak fixes in place – Because our measurement systems are less sensitive than they should be due to process aggregation, it would be tough to tell if a given fix was having the desired effect even if the data was available in trend form. Better designed measurement systems can show us if a fix is working or not, but we often fail to track errors at the process level – we only track the big problems. That's sad, because we waste a lot of limited time attempting to fix common, nagging problems with weak fixes that are unfortunately all too common as well (such as verbal reminders and longer procedures).

Measures and trending are not used to understand and improve systems

The Hammer

Cultural Challenge	We try to use measures to control people instead of improve systems
First Step	Use balanced scorecards and trending to understand all key processes
Leverage Point	Teach all employees to read behavior curves and identify system impacts
Key Tools	Vital signs, scorecards, trend lines and limits, performance summary database

Why do most organizations measure the things that they do? If you could go back in time, what would the genesis of your existing measurement practices be? The cultural norm, in almost all organizations, is to measure the performance – the output – of people and machines. After all, they are the ones that we are paying money to or for. We need these output measures to help us make sure that we are getting what we paid for. These measures also help us project how much more we can make, and in turn sell, to others.

Unfortunately, this skewed approach to systems measurements has led to work cultures that also primarily focus on output – this is one reason why it is so difficult for many companies to make the shift towards a dominant customer focus. When companies were smaller, it was more common to measure at the process level – organizational layers were fewer.

To gauge where your current work culture stands relative to balanced performance measurement and improvement, consider the following questions:

- When you review performance in a meeting, which performance measures are first on the agenda? Which ones are reviewed with the most emotion attached to them? Which measures don't, or rarely, get discussed at all?

- What types of performance are tracked, measured, and trended on a daily basis? Which areas are only looked at monthly or quarterly? What types of measures are not even tracked, but should be?

- If you asked your front line people to tell you which measures matter the most to management, what would they say? Which measures would the highest percentage of people mention, and which measures might be rarely mentioned, if they are mentioned at all?

- If someone walked around your facility, which performance areas would they notice are being emphasized and tracked? If an analysis of your computer system or spreadsheet files was performed, what would the person doing such analysis think was most important to your organization?

8

Measurement System Weaknesses

- Measures are mainly used as a hammer
- Main KPI focus is on aggregated, outcome counts
- Alignment between daily work and KPI effect is low
- Few process specific measures are trended over time
- Groups struggle to build theories from trends
- Process variation is not understood
- Process capability is rarely considered
- Mixed measures make process analysis difficult
- Few groups capture daily process errors and defects
- Data capture and analysis take too much time

The Hammer

Poor measures

Few trends

Reactive behaviors

Most, if not all, organizations measure something. Unfortunately, a very small percentage of organizations have what I would consider to be a high performance measurement system. Some organizations measure too many things, or focus primarily on those numbers that they are required to track in order to satisfy regulatory and legal requirements. Others tend to focus only on certain input and output numbers, such as those related to sales revenue generated, total customers served, total expenses, and total units produced. Very few organizations trend their performance information in an effort to understand their work systems better.

My 30 plus years of experience have led me to conclude that less than 10% of the organizations out there have high performance measurement systems. My experiences as a national Baldrige Examiner, and as a leader in organizations that aspired to be high performers, have helped me identify what I consider to be the Top Ten Measurement system weaknesses that exist in a majority of the world's factories, hospitals, schools, governmental agencies, and service industries. These are listed in the above graphic.

If you would like to challenge my assumptions, feel free to do so. As you do however, please think about two things. First of all, how well does your existing measurement work? What criteria and factors did you consider as you answered this evaluative question? Secondly, as you read over the list of measurement system weaknesses provided above, which ones sound familiar to you? What negative experiences or waste have you witnessed in the workplace where one or more of the weaknesses might have existed? How much do you need to improve your measurement system, and where are improvements needed?

If you are trying to make your measurement system more effective, putting balanced scorecards in place is a great place to start. In fact, it is one of the first places I would start in terms of making measurement system improvements. Many of our ineffective leadership behaviors and practices are driven by the lack of a balanced look at our work systems. Using balanced scorecards helps you focus on the right things and understand your work systems to a much higher degree. How do you know if you are improving in the right places?

Great Systems!
"Simple systems, great results!"

Measurement System Install Phases

Design It — Select the model and features that you would like your measurement system to have

Build It — Begin installing a framework to support your measurement system design goals

Use It — Use daily data capture, scorecards, and process-focused goals to improve performance

Improve It — At least annually, evaluate and improve the key processes in your measurement system

Building a measurement system involves four key phases:

Select measurement system model and features – We will begin by defining who or what (process or outcome) we will be measuring. Once we know what we are measuring, we can define the vital signs (key measures) that make up the personal, process, site, or business unit scorecards. Finally, we can decide how, and if, we want to connect our measurement system to our recognition, performance review, compensation, and personal development systems, among others.

Install a framework to support design goals – Once the design parameters have been defined, we can begin to install the different components of our measurement system. Scorecards have to be designed for different work groups, data capture devices and forms need to be created, and performance goals have to be set and integrated into our performance management processes. The choice of using pilot groups, versus rapid and full deployment, must also be made to help determine how fast we need to put our framework in place.

Use the different measurement techniques – One way, like it or not, to determine if you have the right mix of measures is to measure a lot of things, and then find those ratios that are the best indicators of process performance. In other words, *you have to use your measures to find out how to improve your measures.* Fortunately, today's computer hardware and software make this a lot easier to do than it was even 20 years ago. There is a bit of an art to selecting the right measures, but you can't begin to create a masterpiece until you get the brush wet.

Annually evaluate and improve your measure mix, along with your capture and crunch techniques – A measurement system should improve from year to year as part of an annual improvement event that kicks off the annual planning process. It is important to devote a little time yearly to look at what is working, and not working, with each of your key work systems. Typical measurement system changes that are needed each year include improving data capture and crunch techniques, selecting new benchmarks that align more closely with strategy, and enhancing the different forms of visual management we use to share performance results.

10

Common Measure Selection Process

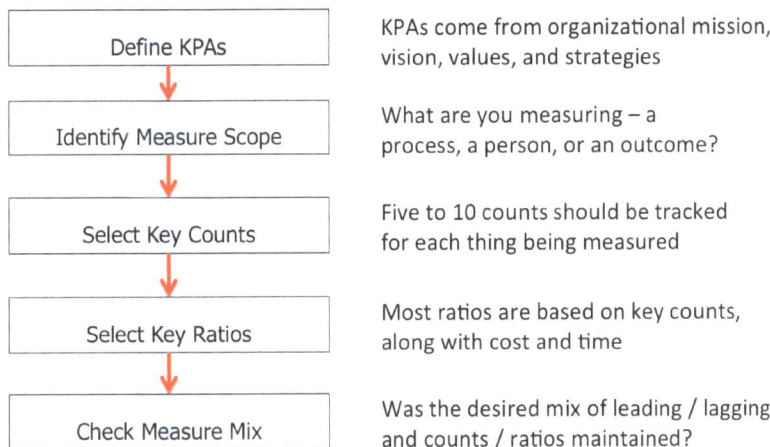

Process Step	Description
Define KPAs	KPAs come from organizational mission, vision, values, and strategies
Identify Measure Scope	What are you measuring – a process, a person, or an outcome?
Select Key Counts	Five to 10 counts should be tracked for each thing being measured
Select Key Ratios	Most ratios are based on key counts, along with cost and time
Check Measure Mix	Was the desired mix of leading / lagging and counts / ratios maintained?

Check Measure Mix - Before you begin executing the above five measure selection steps, you might want to review the measurement system building codes listed on page 13. In most organizations, measurement system designs currently violate several, if not all, of these codes. As you go forward, even if only in an experimental sense, you will need to decide which of these codes you will follow, and which ones you will bend a little on. Your first challenge will arise when you compare your list of existing measures to these building codes and notice the mismatches. For example, rarely are 75% of an organization's key measures leading ratios.

Define Key Performance Areas (KPAs) - Measure selection is our starting point, and it begins with defining the key performance areas (KPAs) of the organization. Typical KPAs are safety, quality, cost, and people for cost centers, with the 'Growth' performance area being added for profit centers (since they have revenue generation roles). Additional KPAs can be added to a scorecard to emphasize a particular performance area (i.e. splitting the Quality KPA into a Service KPA and a Waste KPA, with 2-3 key measures being defined for each).

Identify Measure Scope – Simply put, our current measurement scope, in most cases, is wrong. Silo-based companies have a habit of focusing on outcome measures that fall into KPA buckets. For example, aggregate safety measures for a site are often used to troubleshoot safety concerns, and the goal is to 'Improve Safety' versus improving process performance in general, or the safety systems, that are producing safety results (along with other results). Try to measure at the process level first and then aggregate the numbers outward if you need to – just remember that the measure becomes less sensitive as you aggregate additional teams, sites, and processes (dissimilar systems) together into one measure.

Select Key Counts and Ratios – Try to avoid getting caught up in exactly what your ratios will be. Instead, focus on capturing a well-rounded set of counts (at least five to ten counts per process is typical). *Any count can be converted into a ratio*, so if you have the counts, the ratios can be created. Our problem tends to lie in that we don't capture the counts (often error or defect related) for each key process at all. In turn, we miss out on the chance to trend key performance ratios over time and begin to truly understand our processes.

Great Systems!
"Simple systems, great results!"

What are We Measuring?

Vital signs can be identified for anything, but what do we really want to measure?

Person — People measuring may give one the impression that good measuring is occurring, but are you really measuring the processes that person owns?

Outcome — Outcome measuring is also common, but how often does this practice result in resource competition?

Process — The best approach, but for some reason, the least used – why do people struggle so much to see processes?

Too often we get overly focused on what types of measure to use, or how many measures we should have, instead of first getting clarity about WHAT we are going to measure. For example, focusing primarily on outcome measures will tend to (1) encourage people to play with the numbers and (2) reinforce a silo thinking and acting mentality, since outcomes tend to be department owned. Focusing too much on outcomes also results in 'Rah-Rah" attempts to stop errors that are known, but also accepted – a zero defects promotion would be an example.

At other times, we focus on measuring a person instead of a process. Measuring a person may give you an overall view of their effectiveness if you have the right mix of measures, but such an approach also often gives you only general feedback on the combined performance of a lot of their personal processes. Leverage can be gained by focusing on measuring and improving those work processes and systems that affect personal performance the most on the job, such as meeting effectiveness or project management. *Holding a leader accountable to key process performance measures for the processes they execute is the best practice approach to use.*

Over my thirty plus years of process improvement application and learning (it is a loop you know), I have seen shifts in how measures are used. For example, manufacturers measure things quite well at the process level, but the methods used to crunch the data and use it to drive true system change can still be improved. Service groups however, that are both closer to the customer each day and make up a higher percentage of the total cost picture, measure less at the process level and more at the location level. This business sector also uses weak performance review practices (performance to budget) that were adopted from manufacturing.

To understand and address what is affecting location performance, one must have a well-rounded set of process level ratios at hand. Also, it is key that daily error and defects are systematically captured as well – if not, problem diagnosis and system fixing will be more challenging. *The right data must exist to allow for the exploration of the relationship between error rates and process outcomes.*

Measurement System Building Codes

- 75% of top KPIs are leading ratios

- 100% tracking of errors and defects at the process level

- All vital signs are trended monthly

- Goal mix of 25% absolute and 75% (or better) leading ratios

- 75% linkage between profit sharing measures and daily actions

Cutting corners on building codes leads to a weaker measurement system

Building codes are rules that need to be followed in order to help ensure that building integrity is maintained and a safe building is erected. Violate a building code, and that portion of the building's infrastructure will be compromised. For example, for a concrete patio to last, rebar needs to set into the concrete. Also, the concrete needs to be poured to a minimum depth. Violate one, or both, building codes and the patio will begin showing cracks much sooner than you expected.

Building a measurement system is no different, but the cracks in a poorly designed measurement system are difficult, if not impossible, to see unless you really know where to look. For example, most measurement systems are faulty in the sense that they use lagging counts as the primary type of key performance indicator. Lagging counts are bad for two reasons. First, as they are counts instead of ratios, there is no relationship between the count and the system that produced that data. An expenditure of $10,000 in the Recognition cost center means little unless you know how many people that recognition affected or at least how many awards were given out. Ratios show cause and effect, whereas counts merely show that something happened.

Second, lagging indicators look backwards instead of forwards. They tell you where you have been, but they are not indicators of where your processes are taking you. It make take months before a system change becomes visible in a lagging indicator, and there is a high likelihood that other process changes will offset the expected effects of that change by that time.

Another big design flaw in most measurement systems is that they only measure at the macro level – at the business unit, site, or department level. None of those three groups directly produce results, as they are a collection of processes. Best in class measurement systems measure from the inside out – they start at the process level and roll up to the department, site, and higher levels. In addition to measuring at too high of a level, we also often make the mistake of looking at monthly trends for only a few measures, and rely on making table-based 'snapshot' comparisons as our diagnostic data source for most process troubleshooting efforts.

Great Systems!
"Simple systems, great results!"

Measurement System Design Goals

Why should you build a better measurement system?

✓ Reduce costs by eliminating non-value added activities

✓ Increase process ownership and cost understanding

✓ Develop a strong linkage between workgroup and company goals

✓ Improve internal and external customer service

✓ Move towards balance between key performance areas

✓ Create a higher level of systems understanding and engagement

Keep the process simple, focused, and flexible

Hopefully you can recognize the danger in relying primarily on manpower reduction or an efficiency increase emphasis to improve performance. If you choose such a route however, you will give up any chance of obtaining consistent employee cooperation in your improvement efforts (why work to improve if jobs are going to be lost!). Instead, emphasize the need to improve all key areas of performance and appreciate the balance between key metrics.

You will also lose business over time as internal and external customer needs go unmet. People try to make the "most important" numbers look good in one area at the expense of others. A key goal of your measurement system design efforts is to have a balanced set of measures on your dashboards and scoreboards – create the right perception of what the important numbers are.

The objectives of achieving measurement system and decision making balance are quite broad. While they represent the end result of what you should strive to accomplish, more sharply defined goals are also needed. The following six goals were therefore established to help you focus on the desired outcomes from your redesigned measurement system.

- Reduce costs by eliminating non-value added activities
- Create process ownership by implementing the concepts of "open book management" -- teach everyone about the costs of doing business
- Develop a strong linkage between company and process team goals
- Improve internal and external customer service
- Ensure that balance is maintained between various performance areas
- Create a greater systems understanding among all employees

Attaining these goals may seem like an insurmountable task, but I feel that this system is not only designed to meet them, but it is also designed as a simple way for doing so. My experience with performance measurement in the past had given me a good idea of what did not work, and why. In most cases, the biggest challenge is to accept the fact that traditional performance improvement approaches that are commonly promoted as "the right thing to do" are actually lacking in several areas. A more effective approach is needed.

14

Key Book Concepts

Vital Signs	Scorecards	Goals
Design	Build	Use	Improve
Capture	Crunch	Change

The key to accelerating daily process performance improvement

The basic process for building better work systems – just like building a house

The key to accelerating daily process performance improvement

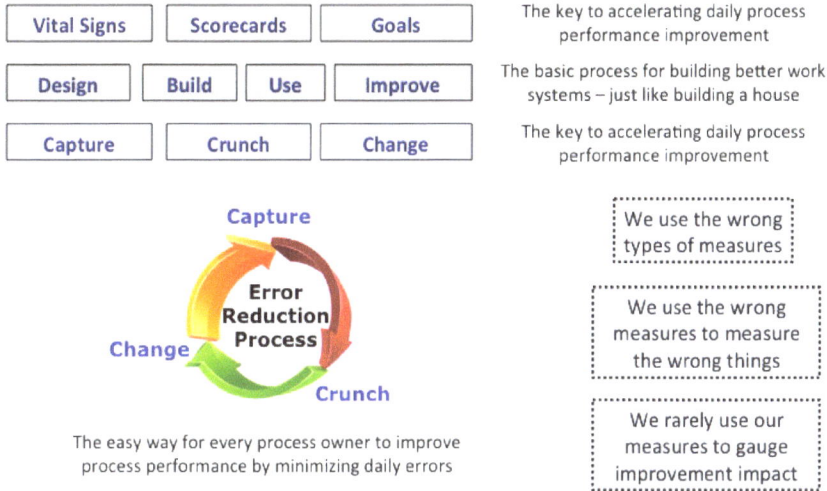

Capture

Error Reduction Process

Change

Crunch

The easy way for every process owner to improve process performance by minimizing daily errors

We use the wrong types of measures

We use the wrong measures to measure the wrong things

We rarely use our measures to gauge improvement impact

In short, I can sum up the main measurement system design and use mistakes made by a high percentage of organizations into three main areas:

We use the wrong types of measures – Simply put we rely too heavily on lagging counts to gauge how well we are performing. It is bad enough to depend on lagging indicators more than leading indicators (what Dr. Deming called 'driving by using the rear view mirror with the windshield papered over'). We make matters much worse however when we use lagging counts as our primary type of measure. Counts don't provide a connection between the measure and the system being measured – no ratio equals no relationship. Sadly, any count can be converted into a ratio by using time or dollars as a divisor, or by using a percentage of total.

We measure the wrong things – The prevailing norm is to measure at the company, business unit, or site level, instead of relying mainly on process-based measures. Measures that are not process-based lose their relative value quite quickly because they represent an aggregation of multiple processes or work systems. Lumping measures from different processes together can either introduce extra variation or washout (hide) excessive variation that might exist in one system versus another. Fewer calculations might be needed to create these higher level measures, but at the same time, decision quality will suffer significantly. Bad decisions in turn, result in limited time and financial resources being used to make changes that are less value added. It is better to roll into these measures using process-based measures as the foundation.

We use our measures in the wrong way – Most people use measures to monitor other people – to hold them accountable in layman's terms. Measures SHOULD be used to predict future process performance, to determine if improvements are having the desired impact, and to identify high leverage opportunities for change. We might think that we are using measures to track whether improvement is occurring or not, but when we use the wrong measures (lagging counts) and fail to measure at the process level, we are only fooling ourselves.

The practices and tools presented in this book will help you avoid the above problems and make better resource investment decisions. Sound measurement practices will also help you accelerate your improvement efforts.

Great Systems!
"Simple systems, great results!"

NOTES

Design It!

BLUE PRINT

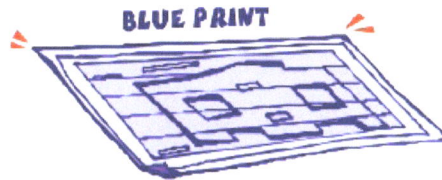

Making Measurement System Design Choices

- Define processes to be monitored
- Define key performance areas (KPAs)
- Identify key counts and ratios
- Develop measurement definitions and procedures

Designing any key work system is much like designing a house. With each component of the house, you have to make foundation, framing, wiring, roofing, interior, and other choices. Similarly, when you build a measurement system, you have to define processes, select the process vital signs, assemble them into scorecards, decide who will measure what and how often, and perhaps most importantly, decide how you will use the data to make key decisions.

The system recommended here was not assembled by chance, or merely copied from those that others had tried. Instead, it represents an evolutionary effort to take the successful aspects of traditional performance measurement systems and marry them with innovative changes that can help avoid existing shortcomings. This system has been tested, and works, in multiple settings, including those of a health care, service, and manufacturing nature.

Effective performance measurement should serve as the cornerstone of your design effort. By "effective", I mean that you should strive to avoid the traditional performance measurement flaws -- singular focus on certain measures, ineffective goal setting, and a lack of appreciation for system (process) capability. Most importantly, you should try to avoid using the performance measurement results as a "hammer", which is a tactic used in many companies.

Two key actions should be taken to help support this need. First, workshops should be held to help define what effective measurement is, and what it is not. Second, goals should NOT be established without first knowing what the capabilities of the work system are AND identifying the actions that will be taken to impact performance. For example, avoid simply setting goals that are ten percent higher than the year before (a common business practice).

The concept of balanced scorecards provides the starting point. By selecting a set of key performance areas for your company, you can, in turn, ask each work group to select the most meaningful measures (vital signs) that they can influence within each area. Selecting the areas and measures however is only the first step. You need to follow up this effort by setting performance baselines, defining system capabilities for each measure, establishing possible performance improvement actions, and finally, setting goals per the expected changes.

Great Systems!
"Simple systems, great results!"

Why is This Approach Different?

⭐ Daily data capture is mandatory

⭐ Cost focus is included

⭐ All key processes have scorecards

⭐ Focus on meaningful leading ratios

⭐ All process team members are engaged

Build the process into each person's daily job

The approaches presented in this book are intended to be different than those presented in mainstream articles and books on the topics of measurement and balanced scorecards. This difference is largely due to the fact that these approaches have evolved from traditional practices as they were repeatedly tested and modified s in multiple fields of practice.

The following paragraphs highlight what are considered to be the five unique aspects of this measurement approach.

Daily Lean Data Capture -- The reporting process itself needs to be very simple, but it also needs to be daily and process-based. Because this system is to be used at the process / work team level, you need to "chunk up" the data collection needs so you don't overburden any one person. By focusing on only the key counts to be captured for each work team / process, the list of numbers to regularly watch and chart does not become overwhelming. Lastly, the use of pre-designed paper forms, spreadsheet templates, or tablet applications, helps avoid having to create a lot of "computer experts" to support visual management and other reporting needs.

Include a Cost Focus to Inspire Open Book Ownership -- As long as misconceptions about costs, profits, and who gets what exist, it will be difficult to gain widespread ownership of any process improvement effort. Leaders of such efforts have found that once teams begin to realize success, they also recognize that someone is financially benefiting from the gains. Unless such benefits extend to some degree throughout the organization, skepticism will gain a greater and greater foothold on the attitudes of each employee as money is saved.

In the long run, all employees should see some form of financial gain for their efforts. *More importantly, people will be more motivated to make improvements if they (1) know what waste costs and (2) feel like it is some of their own money that is being wasted each day.* You don't have to share the exact financial data – rounding and percent of total use actually improves understandability. I have seen, on multiple occasions, the changes in behavior that come with an enhanced understanding of what daily process waste and poor service cost the organization.

Design Features

Lean Data Capture

Increased Cost Understanding

Balanced Scorecards

Meaningful Measures

Full Team Engagement

Blend traditional performance measurement with innovative changes

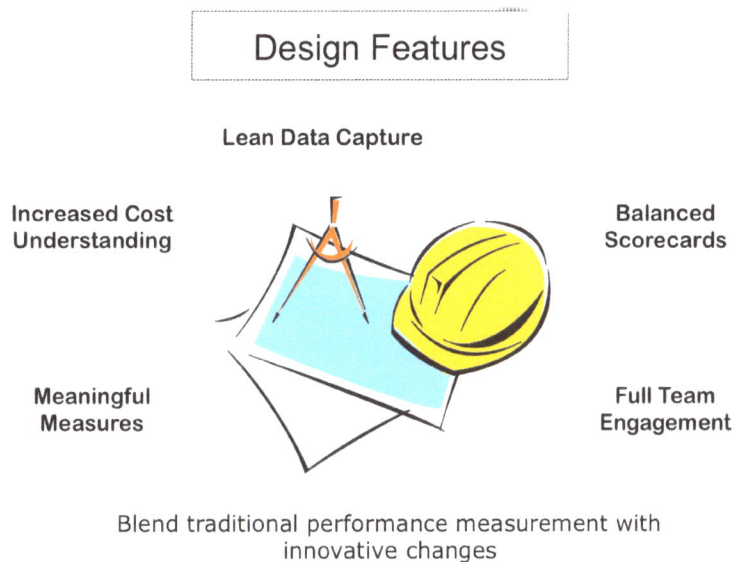

All Processes Have Scorecards – Measurement practices, such as the balanced scorecard approach, work the best when (1) all process teams at a location are involved and (2) a balanced set of measures has been defined for each process. People may wish to track additional measures, but a basic set of key counts (and by default, ratios) should be defined for each process in a manner that is consistent with the design criteria for the measurement system as a whole. Some processes may not cycle fast enough to have measures that change daily, but **meaningful leading ratios can, and should, be defined for any process**.

Practical, Meaningful Measures -- People are rarely motivated by measures that do not fairly represent the work they do, or that are largely out of their influence, no matter what types of changes they try to make (at least ethically). Similarly, *more leadership credibility is lost, versus motivation gained, when people are routinely challenged to achieve goals that exceed the current process capability of the processes they own*. If you involve your process owners in the selection of process-based measures that they can influence, and that are targeted at improving a balanced set of process outcomes, there is a much greater likelihood that these leaders will work to engage their teams in regular process improvement efforts.

The Power of Total Team Engagement -- Conceptually, people will agree that process teams can make an organization more effective. Disagreement begins to surface however as we attempt to define what it actually takes to gain the advantages of empowerment and 100% true engagement (self direction). Answering this second question requires a response that is conditioned by the current culture. If a culture of low trust, weak or adversarial relationships, and 'Do as I say' management exists, it may take years to weaken the negative mental models and create new, positive work practices and beliefs.

The types of measures used, and how they are used, play a key role in shaping an organization's culture. Once people know how their performance will be measured, that it will be measured fairly, and that the captured results will not be used against them, they will begin to look for actions and changes to take to help improve the performance of their workgroup, and in turn, the company. It is key that your employees know how they can convert their ideas for improvement into reality. In short, how can they personally improve the numbers?

Great Systems!
"Simple systems, great results!"

Key Measurement System Design Questions

- How many key processes do we have?

- What are our vital signs for key process performance?

- What do customers expect from our processes?

- How do we capture key transaction details?

- How should we track daily process errors and defects?

- How do we create ownership in process measurement and improvement?

- What approach should we use for formal performance review?

Some of the above measurement system design questions will be answered in this book, as they tend to relate to generic, tested best practices. In other cases, such as "How many key processes do we have?" the answers are dependent on the organization type, size, and focus. They are important questions to ask, but they won't be answered here – you have to follow-up with that activity when you are ready to do so.

Keep in mind that processes should be designed to meet the defined customer requirements. This is not always the case, as some legacy processes are still in use simply because there seems to be no need to change. It is more common however to see process design based on what we think the customer wants versus what our 'voice of the customer' listening posts might be telling us. Begin by defining the process and its key customer (internal or external) requirements. Once you have done that, you can use the practices described later in this book to select those key counts and ratios that best monitor the vital signs of the processes you own.

It is likely that you will need to re-design your formal performance review approach (i.e. monthly meeting focus and reports) so it better meshes with the recommended measurement practices. For example, many organizations review performance monthly simply by comparing monthly cost center counts for different periods of time, or to the budgeted goal. Making such comparisons might be a common practice, but they do not tell us enough about process performance to be truly useful. In fact, comparing an actual count to an expected budget count only really gives you feedback on how well you executed the budget estimating process.

When leading ratios serve as the primary measure type, and trend lines with meaningful control limits exist to visually view process behavior, the performance review effort becomes focused on three key questions. First, what patterns of behavior do we see in each trend line? Second, how well are the process-specific changes we have made working? Finally, what types of future process changes make the most sense as process improvement investments?

A Key System Design Choice

- **Process OR Outcome Focus?**

  Many measure with an outcome focus

  "Here is our safety scorecard"

- **To what degree are outcome results RELATED?**

  Using an outcome focus may result in poorer system results overall

  "How do we decide who gets the money?"

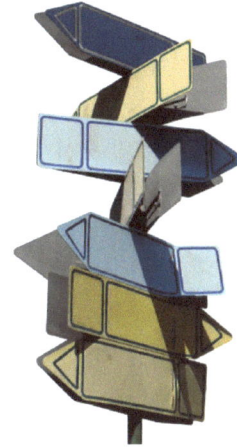

One thing that amazed me about the established energy industry is how outcome focused they were. Over time, their approach began to make sense, even though it is not necessarily an approach that is conducive to sustained, best in class results. Most companies that still focus on outcome, versus process, measures also still have silos within their organization.

The Safety department works to improve safety outcomes, the HR department focuses on people outcomes, and the Finance department makes changes to affect financial outcomes. That is how the jobs are designed. The approach works, but it does not really encourage teamwork across departments. Worse yet, when we focus on trying to improve an outcome measure, we tend to use weaker system changes such as reminders, slogans, and quotas.

We should be focusing on the process, and improving the outcome measures for EACH process through process improvement. This 'inside out' approach has been proven to be one of the fastest methods for driving culture change and accelerated process improvement. It is not used that much because of the degree of change it requires. For example, to support each process owner's job changes related to new measurement responsibilities, measurement and compensation systems should be redesigned. One reason this approach works well is that essentially *everyone's job is designed to require a focus on the daily processes they are responsible for, and integrated monitoring systems exist to provide real time process feedback*.

Evidence of the success of this concept can be most easily found in the sports world. College coaches like John Wooden and Nick Saban have achieved repeated success by teaching their players to focus on the process, and let the outcomes take care of themselves. This did not mean that each coach did not expect perfection – it was quite the contrary. They expected 'process execution' perfection however – they knew outcome perfection would follow.

The rule itself is simple, but not enough people follow it in a disciplined manner:

Focus on reducing process defects, and more importantly process errors, for every process, and a variety of performance outcomes will be positively affected.

Great Systems!
"Simple systems, great results!"

Our Basic Need for Balance

What is Balance?

- A state of equilibrium
- To bring into harmony or proportion
- To counteract the effect of another weight or force

Where is It Needed for Success?

- Almost any type of sport
- Lifestyle – work, family, play
- Business
- Nature

Few systems in life will function properly if they are out of balance. Most of these systems we take for granted, such as the biological systems in nature and the ten key systems within our own bodies. With physical fitness systems, such as the game of football team or weightlifting, we understand the importance of balance, but we often fail to make the connection between these 'not our kind of business' examples and our work world.

In all of these cases, including work, *balance is essential for sustained high performance.*

Work systems get out of balance when we focus too much on what is most tangible or what seems to be the most important. Overemphasizing the need for improved short-term measure performance can also throw our work systems out of balance, and compromise long-term goals over time. A poorly designed measurement system will encourage both intended, and unintended, workplace behaviors that can throw a process or system out of balance, and even make it spin out of control. Conversely however, balanced measurement systems and job designs can lead to effective, focused, and productive workplace beliefs and behaviors on the part of all employees.

The most common out of balance situation in the world of work exists where too much emphasis in placed on production or output, as opposed to quality or safety. We may often say that all three of these performance areas are important, but when you look at how we measure, behave, and make decisions, you can often detect a significant lack of balance.

Establishing the connection between balanced process performance results and the daily efforts of each employee is key. Do your employees see the connection between their daily jobs and the success of the organization? How do they know what measures are important? Do the various performance measures used throughout your organization complement each other, or do you have conflicting performance goals in some areas? Poorly linked measurement systems will throw a system out of balance, just as the daily actions of good intentioned, but poorly informed, employees will. The tools in this book will help you establish clearer and stronger 'work to result' connections, and help restore performance balance.

Can You Run with the Bulls?

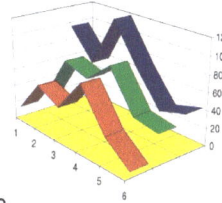

Statistical Advantage	Winning Percentage		
	'98-99	'97-98	'96-97
Turnovers	58.8	58.4	60.3
Rebounds	65.2	65.2	64.3
Field Goal Percentage	78.2	80.0	80.5
Rebounds & Turnovers	78.5	79.8	80.7
FG Pct. & Rebounds	88.0	87.8	90.1
FG Pct. & Turnovers	89.4	91.9	89.7
All Three	95.7	98.2	97.9

What 2-3 measures best predict your chances for success?

Balance is consistently measured and analyzed in the world of sports at a much greater level than it normally is in the world of work. Perhaps this difference is related to the high salaries that players make or the significant revenue streams that sports generate. Why balance is analyzed to a much greater degree however is not what is important – the level of systems understanding and improvement that occurs as a result of this measurement and analysis is.

In a now ancient issue of *ESPN the Magazine*, the above analysis was presented to help explain why the Chicago Bulls had such a dominant basketball team in the late 1990s. While it would be convenient and easy to attribute their success to Michael Jordan, the facts show that both teamwork and a focus on several key dimensions of 'on the court' performance is what really made the difference. In short, the Bulls were successful primarily because they excelled in three key areas that are critical for basketball success – rebounds, shooting percentage, and turnovers. What are your vital signs – your critical indicators of process excellence?

Note that when the Bulls beat their opponent in all three categories, their winning percentage was the highest. In those cases where they only had a rebounding edge – the other team surpassed them relative to low turnovers and high shooting percentage – their winning percentage was significantly lower than when they excelled in two or all three areas.

While this might only seem logical to you, think about your own organization. **What 4-5 measures best predict your chances of success?** Once you have defined these vital signs – and many organizations have not done this analysis yet – check to see if you are measuring and trending those metrics on a consistent basis, and in particular, relative to your competition.

Believe it or not, there are organizations out there that only measure and trend OUTPUT results on a consistent basis – they look at other key results on only a snapshot basis, if at all. At the same time, they struggle to explain why they just can't seem sustain high levels of performance.

Great Systems!
"Simple systems, great results!"

The Efficiency – Service Tradeoff

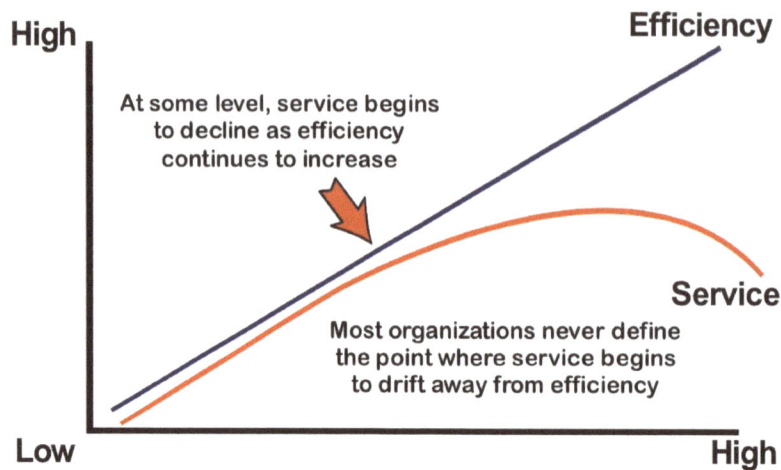

High | **Efficiency**

At some level, service begins
to decline as efficiency
continues to increase

Service

Most organizations never define
the point where service begins
to drift away from efficiency

Low | **High**

Over the past thirty plus years, many organizations have experimented with the concept of work teams, only to experience less then satisfactory results. Similarly, attempts have been made to put total quality, re-engineering, lean manufacturing, or six sigma programs or processes in place, with the same degree of limited success. In each case, a key ingredient was often missing -- *a strong connection between the concept of continuous improvement and how one actually "lives" their job each day across all employee groups.*

Growth, cost increases, profit margin declines, and changing customer expectations are not unique to any industry. It seems as if these business challenges become more pervasive each day. Such has been the case in the service and manufacturing organizations where the techniques and tools described in this workbook have been implemented. Without meaningful, process-based measurement systems in place, it would have been difficult to stay ahead of these challenges and sustain the business growth rates that we did.

In order to remain competitive and maintain, or move towards, a position of market leadership, you need to have a performance measurement system in place that will complement the efforts of your process (work) teams. To make changes quickly, you need to optimize the time that you choose to invest in your performance improvement efforts. To ensure that buy-in and ownership is created and maintained, true empowerment is a must. Lastly, in order to meet the ever-changing expectations of your customers, you somehow need to balance the seemingly opposing goals of service quality versus efficiency. A meaningful measurement system tells you how well you are achieving these goals. No feedback, no motivation to change.

It is often this last objective that proves to be the most daunting. Many, if not most, organizations are culturally conditioned to focus on cost savings, especially in the area of labor. As these types of savings are the most tangible, they are also the most tempting. Even in those companies whose reputation has been built on customer service, shrinking margins are rapidly encouraging them to compromise service for the more immediate, and often short term, financial benefits that reducing, or at least "controlling", manpower seem to provide. When such decisions are made, quality, morale, and safety performance usually decline, whether the organization has the measures in place to recognize these declines in performance or not.

GWS Building Code!

Are You Normal?

→ Most processes are normally distributed (bell curve)

→ Sigma is a measure of variation around the average

→ "In control" processes are predictable

Mean or Average

-1 σ   +1 σ

60 to 75%
90 to 98%
99 to 100%

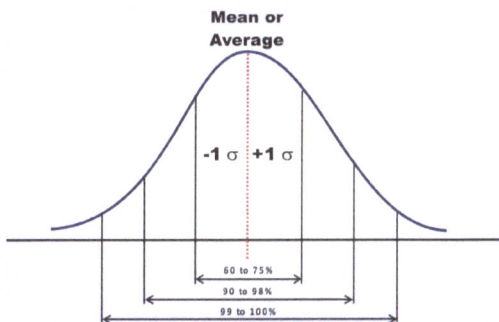

Process Improvement Goals
1. Reduce variation
2. Shift the average

"Don't hammer people for common cause variation, but do expect variation to tighten over time."

A key role of management is being able to predict what a system or process will do. Once a supervisor or manager can predict what their systems will do in a fact-based manner, they will also have a better idea of what their systems are capable of. As fundamental system changes are made to improve the system or process, the control charts for the affected measures should reflect the success of those changes – in particular, variation (process width) should decrease.

Most processes are normally distributed - certain percentages of its produced values fall within certain distances from the average. This measure of standard deviation (also known as sigma) is used to describe these distances. In normally distributed systems, 99 to 100% of the values will fall within a process width of six standard deviations (three on one side of the average and three on the other). Completing a control chart for a given process metric will help you learn more about the relationships that exist between process width and measure predictability.

One common area of failure occurs when customer specifications do not match up with what the system is capable of providing. For example, if an emergency room promises to treat all patients within 45 minutes after they arrive at the hospital, the value of 45 minutes should be three standard deviations greater than the process average. If it is not, customer expectations will not be met a certain percentage of the time.

Similarly, if the sales force promises the customer that a part will have a tolerance of plus or minus one inch, the actual process width of the system should be no wider than this amount. Most people only have a general sense of what their systems are capable of providing, because they have not done the measurement and charting. As a result, they make promises to get new business, and hope that others will find a way to meet the expectations of these new customers, and in turn, keep them. Sadly, they often end up wondering why their customers disappeared.

The moving range formula for control limits will work fine for most of the measures you will want to construct control charts for. Reference the works of Donald Wheeler for more 'easy to understand' information on variation and using the moving range formula to measure it.

Great Systems!
"Simple systems, great results!"

GWS Building Code!

When Should Limits be Changed?

Began trending and posting changeover times and delays

Began holding changeover improvement team meetings

Began using changeover ready tool and part carts

Where SHOULD the limits have been changed?

HINT: Look for 2-3 change points

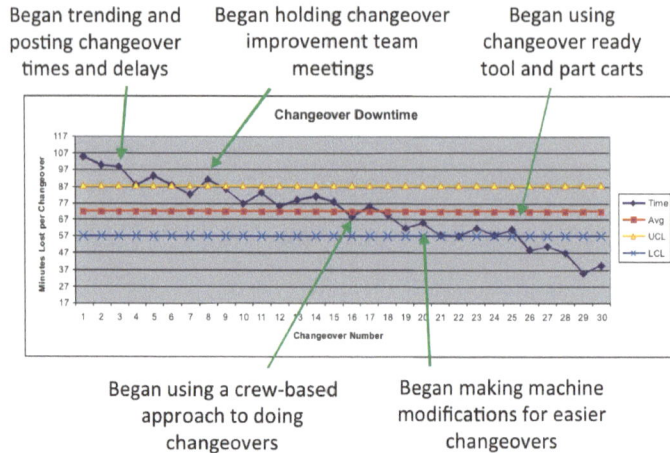

Changeover Downtime

Began using a crew-based approach to doing changeovers

Began making machine modifications for easier changeovers

Change limits when the data tells you to!

It is always fun to ask a professed quality person, and in particular, a certified six sigma black belt or master black belt, the simple question presented at the top of this page. A small percentage of people will give you the 'right' answer, which is "when the data tells you to." More commonly, people will tell you that they change their control limits (1) every quarter or new operating year when new goals are set, (2) monthly as new data is entered, or (3) we don't have to because we rarely go outside of the limits – they always change as we enter new data.

You might also hear a close to right answer, which is 'whenever the system changes.' As the graphic on the next page indicates, it can be tough to determine when a system change actually does occur. Some changes are obvious – if I install a new electronic medical records system to replace paper charting, my trend lines will shift. My error rates could also be affected however in a slow, erosive way by low morale that is much harder to detect.

Also realize that many of your existing results consist of aggregate data – multiple locations, departments, service lines, etc. – and in turn, reflect a higher or lower level of variation than you might be used to from the process itself. I like to divide sigma (one standard deviation) by the mean (average) to obtain a 'percent sigma' ratio that I use as an indicator of process width. When you are trying to machine a valve to a tight tolerance, the percent sigma will be a very low percentage. I have seen percent sigma rates of 50% and higher however for other non-production processes, such as car rental and quick serve restaurant checkout process times.

Finally, just as it is important to focus on process measures more than outcome measures, it is also key that you focus on reducing process variation to a much greater degree than trying to shift the process average. In most cases, *the process average will move in the right direction on its own if you put effective corrective actions in place for the true root causes of common, daily errors and defects.*

When Does a System Change?

Baseball player	Months between seasons
Pipefitter	Weeks or evenings between shifts
Hotel Check-In Clerk	Hours between shifts
Retail Clerk	Breaks or lunch during shift

When a person leaves, and then returns to work, does the system change?

How much do process outcomes vary before and after lunch break?

When does a system change? I was first taught in statistical process control that you change the control limits when the system changes. Now, I learned SPC within a manufacturing context – applying SPC outside of manufacturing is a little different, as I would later learn. Because I learned SPC in manufacturing, I was more accustomed to seeing process control, as opposed to process improvement, charts. I expected the values captured from the process to stay within the control limits. We would not change those limits until the customer specifications changed, the production equipment changed, or the rate of throughput changed – very tangible things.

What I did not know was that many of my performance measures – my process vital signs – were not sensitive enough to pick up the effects of more subtle system changes. For example, I was only looking at waste, instead of also looking at the human errors that were creating each waste type. Also, as this was a manufacturing process, it was easier to keep machines in control versus people. As I moved into the service process improvement arena, the degree that employee efforts impacted the customer grew, so my measures had to gain sensitivity. As they did, the impact of more human-based system changes on error rates became more evident.

People are not robots, and because they are not 100% programmable, they are affected by what they experience outside of work. One could argue, in turn, that your work processes produce varying results to some degree with every shift change simply because your employees spend 65% of their life outside of work, and they leave the workplace every day for sixteen or so hours. An argument one has during break could affect the quality of the service they provide after the break is over. Our work systems, and the inputs into those systems, are changing all of the time – the key is to define when significant systems change has occurred.

The point is not to argue about when a system changes. Accept that it does and let your data tell you when a change is significant – when the control limits need to be changed. Also, look for evidence of shifts in your results as process improvements are made. If your measures are sensitive enough (process-based and error-focused), you should at least be able to see variation being reduced as the process becomes more consistent and predictable.

Great Systems!
"Simple systems, great results!"

A System Change Example

Consider these facts about Coors Field in Colorado:

- ➤ The Rockies have used 61 pitchers in four years
- ➤ No starter has pitched all four years without injury / minor assignment
- ➤ Very few "1-2-3" or "ten pitch" innings
- ➤ No games to-date with a 1-0 score
- ➤ Only six game winners have scored fewer than four runs

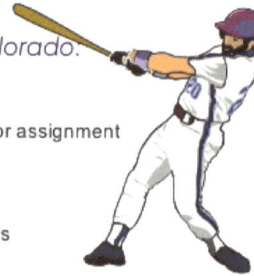

Each year the Rockies lead the league in:

- ➤ Batting average
- ➤ Runs scored
- ➤ Hits per game
- ➤ Home runs
- ➤ Runs Batted In

Home	Away
13.7	**8.8**
Runs per game	Runs per game

What makes this system different from other ballparks?

When I was serving as Director of Quality for Oak Harbor Freight Lines, I used this sports example to help illustrate how different systems produce different results. Eighteen different freight terminals made up our freight system, with some terminals located in urban areas and some located in very rural areas. The tendency was to view all terminals somewhat as equals when it came to performance analysis – the same goals existed for all locations, regardless of employee count, customer type, freight volumes, or terminal location. Terminals were compared against each other, even if their customer groups and freight types were quite different.

From the outside looking in, this might seem like a rather unfair means of gauging performance progress and motivating higher levels of performance – and it is – but I would not be surprised to find that similar 'unfair' comparisons are being made in your own organization. Human struggle to see systems and identify how distinctions in system design can affect system outcomes. It seems easier to think all systems are basically the same, everything averages out over time, and that our people will find a way to do anything if we challenge them.

Sometimes, sports analogies work. In the late 1990s, the Colorado Rockies were one of 28 teams in Major League Baseball (MLB). Their performance was gauged by the same metrics that all of the other 27 baseball teams used. The Rockies' ballpark however was different, and altitude was not the only thing that made this baseball system produce different results than other ballparks. The park was also designed with deep power alleys, for example.

Whether these differences were good or not depends on your perspective. If you like more runs scored per game, then you would like Coors Field. If you preference was for low scoring pitching duels however, you might want to frequent a difference ballpark. Even after a humidor began being used to adjust for elevation differences, pitchers continued to give up more runs at Coors.

By exploring the differences in this baseball system versus the others, and then doing the same for your own work system, you can better understand how **system design affects system output**. In other words, you learn that systems give you what they are designed to give you.

It's Not Just the Altitude?

Physical Differences ...

➤ The altitude -- 5,280 feet up

➤ Deeper gaps (420'+ in left and right field)

➤ Less gravity -- less resistance -- less movement

How can you relate this example to our freight system?

Help Create ...

Behavior Differences

➤ Fear of pitching at Coors

➤ Ego destruction -- poor pitching stats

➤ Stress -- need to be perfect

There are two types of process improvement that measures should reflect – year over year improvement and performance versus a comparable benchmark. Certain outcome measures will improve up to a certain level, but then a plateau is encountered. Many mistake this plateau – this flattening out of performance - to be mental, and in some cases it is. More often than not however, such plateaus are simply the best (or worst) a system can give you based on its design. *All work systems have performance limits that are based on the design of the system.*

The dimensions of Coors Field contributed to increased scoring per game and lower pitcher earned run averages (ERAs) as much as the higher altitude in general did. Once a precedent – a mental model if you will – began to be set for Coors Field being 'a bad place to pitch', the physical system differences began to spawn mental, both perceived and real, differences. This same thing happens daily in organizations, but we just don't see it.

One sales team or maintenance group seems to perform at a lower level in comparison to their 'peers.' Instead of exploring how their work systems might be different in design, and in turn prone to producing different results, we simply label them as 'poor performers' and over time, almost expect them to be the reason we can't get better as an organization.

There is nothing wrong in expecting to see improvement in process vital signs over time. The type of improvements one expects however may need some adjustments. Just as your heartbeat and blood pressure should only be maintained within certain ranges, work systems also exhibit similar behaviors. There are limits to both improvement and decay.

This is why meaningful measurement is so important. Without meaningful measures, you really can't tell how well, or how poorly, a process is performing. You run a much greater risk of making poor decisions relative to investing in a process or trying to improve process performance. This is one of the key reasons improved analytics are being used by more teams to evaluate talent in baseball – different systems produce different results, and our measures help us identify, learn from, and sometimes, benefit from these unique system designs.

Great Systems!
"Simple systems, great results!"

System Change Examples

Consistent Process Mix
Changing Team Mix
Impact of systems change?

Changing Process Mix
Changing Team Mix
Impact of systems change?

Consistent Process Mix
Consistent Team Mix
No systems change?

Changing Process Mix
Consistent Team Mix
Impact of systems change?

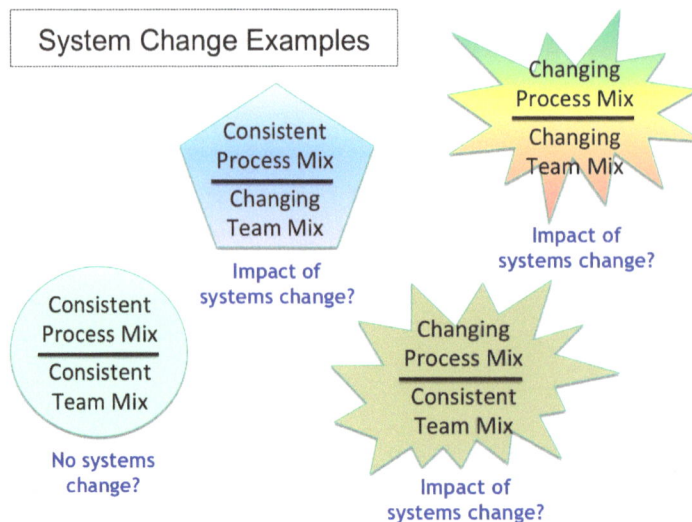

In most workplaces, two main types of systems change – shifts in process mix (work scope) and shifts in team mix (membership) - affect process performance. Team mix refers to the consistency of membership and skill levels. As team members come and go, group dynamics and skill levels shift, and process results are affected to some degree. We may not have measures to prove this relationship exists or to show that the results were affected by these changes, but shifts in sports team chemistry provide an example to consider.

Process mix refers to the mix of products and/or services provided by the team. A construction team might perform five main types of work – five main processes. Each process might have sub-processes, but usually this level of breakdown is not necessary. If a crew does multiple type of work in a day, their potential for error goes up, as the same set of mental models cannot be relied on for the entire work shift.

Because we cannot currently measure the mental effects of changes in team make-up or service offerings, we tend to downplay, if not ignore, the effects themselves. Achieving process excellence however requires sustaining great results over time, and this is pretty tough to do if both of the above factors are constantly shifting on you. The best strategy is to provide workforce management systems that contribute to high retention rates. That is what the best in class companies do – their work environments, compensation, and recognition systems are very well designed and continue to be improved over time.

Process-based, error-focused leading ratios are the best type of measures for detecting the affects of process (work scope) and team mix shifts. If a measure contains more than one process (such as a department safety measure), it loses sensitivity. By focusing on upstream errors instead of downstream defects, the effect of a given systems change can be seen more quickly (this is the nature of a leading indicator).

These two types of systems change are consistently affecting the processes you own now, to some degree. It does take a little more time to measure errors versus defects because there are more errors out there. The time investment is worth it however if you can better control your team mix and provide job aids and other tools to help meet customer-driven process additions and changes. Proactive human error reduction leads to accelerated process improvement!

Defining Key Performance Areas

Key Performance Area (KPA)	Cost Center	Profit Center
Safety / Environment	X	X
Quality / Service	X	X
Cost / Throughput	X	X
People	X	X
Revenue / Sales		X

Most organizations typically have the same KPA mix

Defining key performance areas is a key first step to take in breaking down silos. When an organization has a department structure, it is easy for people in those departments to begin thinking they are only responsible for a certain set, or type of, of measures. For example, the Human Resources people think they are responsible for all of the people-focused measures, and people in other departments think the same way. That is the problem with silos – processes, and the connections between processes, tend to be ignored.

All processes produce results in at least four common areas, whether you actually measure such results or not. These four common areas are safety, quality, people, and cost. You might use different terms to describe a given performance area, such as Service instead of Quality, but the focus of the results is the same. You also have a revenue generation, or Growth, performance area as well if you have sales personnel, and in turn, sales processes at your site. This is the case in profit centers versus cost centers.

Getting department managers to realize that the processes they own – the processes in their departments – produce results in all key performance areas and that they are responsible for improving those results is a key culture change step. No longer will the Safety department be expected to improve the Accounting department's safety results on their own. Instead, the Safety folks will support the efforts of the Accounting process owner in improving the safety of the various processes used in Accounting to support the larger value stream.

Once your leadership team has selected the terms they want to use for your key performance areas, they will then need to weight them against each other. This is the second key step in moving towards a balanced measurement approach – getting leaders to reach consensus on what the most important performance areas for the company are.

Great Systems!
"Simple systems, great results!"

Example Process Definition Matrix

Value Creation Process Area	Key Customer Requirements	Key Work Processes	Process Vital Signs
New Product Development	Improve product features Develop new products Reduce production costs	Development process Customer listening posts Performance review process	Development cycle time Development cycle cost New product success %
Sales and Marketing	Retain current customers Attract new customers Maintain account accuracy	Account development process Customer targeting process Account updating	Customer retention % Revenue growth % Customer satisfaction index
Customer Service	Prompt response to calls Accurate information Timely information	Order entry process Information retrieval process Complaint resolution process	Call abandonment rate External survey score % calls answered in 10 sec.
Purchasing and Receiving	On time material delivery Cost effective raw materials Performance to specs	Receiving process Material ordering process Supplier management	Material cost per pound Avg. $ in inventory On time delivery %
Production	On time schedule completion Quality product Minimal waste	Preparation Assembly Packaging	Process cost per pound Rework / waste % % production to schedule
Shipping	On time shipments Accurate shipments Prompt order fulfillment	Order assembly Shipment scheduling Order labeling	On time % Order cycle time Shipping accuracy score

In a high performance workplace, each department has a chart similar to the one shown above. Organizations that participate in the national Baldrige Performance Excellence award process normally have two main types of processes – value creation processes and support processes. The above matrix summarizes the value creation processes that are typically found in a manufacturing plant. Similar tables for value creation and support processes in health care, service organizations, or school systems can be easily found by referencing the application summaries on the Baldrige website (www.quality.nist.gov).

Value creation processes are used to add some degree of value to a product or service from the perspective of the internal or external customer. Support processes, such as accounting, human resources, or information technology, exist to support external customer value creation processes. The designs of the process definition matrix are basically the same. After defining the processes themselves, you then identify (1) the key internal or external customer requirements of that process and (2) the measures – the vital signs - that will be used to gauge the degree to which you are meeting, or exceeding, those requirements.

Completing these matrices for all of your key work processes is a key step in deploying the use of balanced scorecards across a site, business unit, or organization. How many processes do you have in your organization? Requiring all process owners to use similar tools and approaches to improve process performance helps reinforce the message that process improvement is a company-wide focus and key job expectation of everyone.

The Process Improvement Process

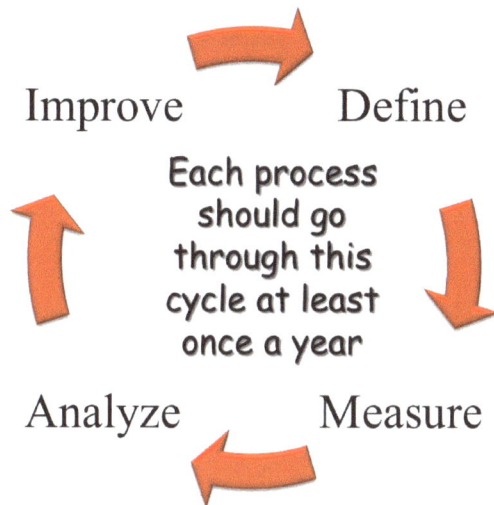

Improve   Define

Each process
should go
through this
cycle at least
once a year

Analyze   Measure

- Hotel Check in
- Customer billing
- Conducting a meeting
- Answering e-mails
- Taking x-rays
- Pouring a foundation
- Conducting RCA
- Getting up each day
- Driving to work
- Holding a tailgate meeting

If you ask someone what the phrase 'process improvement' means to them, you will get a wide variety of responses. In most organizations, formal process improvement involves forming teams to address the biggest problems that the site currently faces. Solving the problem, versus improving the processes that are producing the problem, is the focus. We are focusing on the wrong thing. We are focusing on the outcome instead of the process that is producing the outcome. This misdirected focus often results in a temporary fix that fails over time.

People often struggle to define the key work processes that they own – the main repetitive tasks they do each day as part of their jobs. Such 'process blindness' is partially caused by our tendency to focus on problems first. As Peter Senge stated, "we have been conditioned to respond to events instead of systems." In the above graphic, you will see a list of common, everyday processes. It is likely that one or more of these processes affect you each day. The question is "How often do you measure process effectiveness, capture process errors, and structurally improve process performance?" versus merely capture problems.

I feel safe in stating that most organizations are utilizing only 10% or so of their process improvement capacity. This underutilization is not due to a lack of knowledge, but instead, is driven by an infrastructure that fails to engage enough of the right people who are focusing on the right things. Every process owner should be involving his or her people in formal process improvement on at least an annual basis. Such activities should occur daily, but sadly, some supervisor jobs are not structured to drive actions of this nature.

Process improvement should be built into each leader's job, and in too many cases, it is not. The words are probably in the job description, but the design of the job does not provide enough, if any, time for process analysis and improvement. Improvement may be requested by leaders daily, but rarely are they measured by the specific process improvements they personally lead the implementation of – all leaders own processes!

Great Systems!
"Simple systems, great results!"

GWS Building Code!

The Impact of Mixed Measures

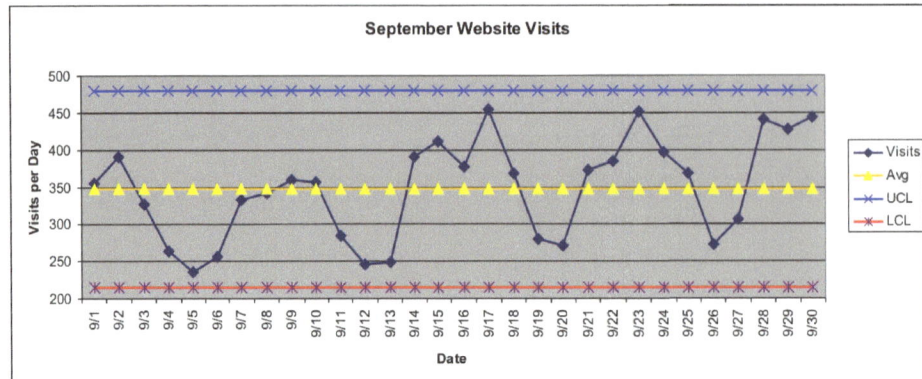

September Website Visits

Most organizations mix systems into one measure – this practice hides both problems and successes!

How effective are the systems you use to measure?

The above table illustrates one of the common measurement mistakes made by organizations each day. In this example, visits to a business website are being trended over time. As you can see, there are peaks and valleys in the data – this is due to weekend data being mixed in with workday data. The shift each weekend from weekend day back to work day is making the variation of the system look greater than it really is for either of the ratios taken separately.

This also commonly occurs with satisfaction survey results. It is for this reason that response rates are important ratios to watch. Survey data with a low response rate is more suspect to bias, as it is harder to get a representative sample with only a 25% response rate unless the sampling plan is well designed and executed. Similarly, the easiest way to improve one's safety results is to hire more people into the relatively lower risk exposure jobs you have. The heavier weighting to the low risk side will automatically make the overall numbers look better.

While ensuring that your measures are process focused may sound logical, it is quite different than the measurement norms that are in use. It is much more common to measure at the site, business unit, or corporate level than at the process level. *Often, only throughout type data is tracked at the process level.* Another common problem is that only sales, production, and safety data is available in trend form at any level – tables of data is the best you can hope for in other performance areas. *All too often, we are failing to measure all of our vital signs, and yet we are trying to effectively diagnose problems and make key decisions.*

It is also easy to get lost in all of the possible measures to use when you are trying to define a set of measures at the site level or higher. A much more efficient approach is to define each process, the requirements for each process, and possible measures to gauge progress in meeting each requirement. As you define possible measures, consider starting with key counts to capture, since any count can be turned into a ratio to provide system relevance to the measure. Without the key counts, meaningful ratios are tough to come by.

System Design Choices Exercise

Identify the key measurement system design choices you need to make, and share your results

Group Dialogue Questions:

- What mix of choices was made?

- What process was used to make them?

    -- What steps, reasons, decision criteria, etc. were used?

- What are the pros and cons of each key system design choice?

Overview	5 minutes
Individual Work	10 minutes
Group Dialogue	20 minutes

35 total minutes

For this exercise, you need to make some measurement system design choices. Here is a summary of some of the key questions that need to be answered:

1. What are our key performance areas?

2. At what level are we going to measure – process, site, business unit …?

3. Who is going to be expected to capture data, and at what frequency?

4. What types of processes are we going to measure? What % of all processes?

5. How should we capture the key errors and effects that occur at the process level each day?

6. How will we create ownership in process measurement an improvement? To what degree will we make process measurement and error tracking mandatory for some positions?

7. How might we need to modify our formal performance review process to take advantage of the new types of data that are available?

Great Systems!
"Simple systems, great results!"

How Many Measures?

In baseball, individual and team performance is measured in three key performance areas. For each area, a variety of key measures are tracked. What measures can you think of?

	Batting	**Pitching**	**Fielding**
I N P U T S	# of at bats At bat outcomes Side of plate used Location hit to Pitch type Pitcher and team Pitcher's hand Time of day Playing surface	# of pitches Pitch type Location Pitch outcome Count	# of attempts Attempt outcome Type of attempt Fielding surface
O U T P U T S	Total hits by type Total bases Total outs by type Total walks Location hit to chart Hitting zone chart	Total pitches Total strikes Total balls Total walks Total strikeouts Total wins and losses Total saves and holds Location chart Hit type totals	Total attempts Total putouts Total assists Total errors
R A T I O S	Batting average On base average Slugging percentage SLOB ratio Strikeout ratio	Earned run average Winning percent Strikes / balls ratio Hits / nine innings	Fielding percent Putouts per game Assists per game

What would a similar chart for your business look like?

What's Your Measure Mix?

Using the baseball example, create a similar chart for your organization or work group. Use the three performance areas that are provided.

	Service	Productivity	Costs
I N P U T S			
O U T P U T S			
R A T I O S			

After completing your chart, circle those items that you currently capture.

Defining Key Work Processes

Key Process	Perf. Area	Customer Requirements	Key Performance Measures
	Safety		
	Quality		
	Cost		
	People		
	Safety		
	Quality		
	Cost		
	People		

Defining Key Work Processes and Measures
Total Time: 55 minutes

Objective: Create a basic key process definition matrix.

Key Questions:
1. What are the key processes that you are responsible for?
2. Who are the customers of these processes, and what are their requirements?
3. What measures will be used to gauge performance to these requirements?

Group Tasks:

1 minute	1. Select roles for the table: scribe / facilitator, timekeeper, reporter.
14 minutes	2. Begin this exercise by selecting a key process – something you are familiar with – to be analyzed. After selecting the process, identify (1) the weight that should be assigned to each of the four performance areas and (2) the key customer requirements of this process.
15 minutes	3. Identify the key safety, quality, people, and cost measures that should be tracked to gauge process effectiveness in meeting these requirements.

Team Report: 3 minutes per team for doing your report out and 10 minutes for the follow-up large group discussion.   *25 total minutes*

As part of the report out, your team should provide an overview of (1) the weightings that were assigned, (2) the customer requirements for the process, (3) the key metrics that were identified, and (4) the process that the team used to reach consensus on the weighting assignments, customer requirements, and key measures that were selected.

Key Process being defined: _____

Performance Area	Weight	Customer Requirements	Key Performance Measures
Safety			
Quality			
People			
Cost			

Great Systems!
"Simple systems, great results!"

NOTES

Build It!

Creating a Framework of Vital Signs, Scorecards, and Goals

- Select leading counts and ratios – process and SBU levels
- Create a daily process scorecard for each process
- Setting KPI goals, weights, and color ranges

If you have ever participated in building a house, you recognize the importance of a sound foundation. If a foundation is designed poorly – too thin of a pour for example – it will fail sooner than expected. Many current measurement systems are flawed in design simply because no one has recognized the design flaws and taken any action to address them. In other cases, people modeled what others were doing to put their own version of the measurement practice in place – right or wrong.

This is why so many groups are failing to use the red-yellow-green color assignments on their scorecards effectively. Someone started out setting the color limits in a less than effective way, and then others simply followed their lead without questioning the current approach or asking if there was a better approach that could be used to set the ranges. As recognition and compensation are often tied to the measures associated with these color ranges, setting them is no arbitrary task. Poor range assignments can lead to significant job dissatisfaction!

Best in class approaches are shared in this book. Several examples and exercises are included to help you avoid making the same mistakes others have made as they designed their measurement systems. Selecting the right mix of measures, with a focus being placed on leading ratios at the process level, is the best place to start, but often the hardest step to effectively make. It is tough to convince people to give their old measures. Without a systems understanding, they don't really worry about what measures are used, as long as their pay or perks don't suffer.

Selecting the right mix of measures is the biggest challenge. The second challenge lies in collecting the data to calculate those measures each day in a lean manner. If it is not easy to collect the data, it will either not be collected, or data integrity will be lost as people make up numbers to get the data quickly and keep you happy. Finally, the manner in which performance ranges (colors) and goals are set, and then weighted and used, will also send strong signals about the intent of the measurement system and the degree to which it is being designed with fair, balanced process measurement in mind.

Great Systems!
"Simple systems, great results!"

Exploring Measure Linkages

COMPANY	External Customer Survey Results Was the customer satisfied?	All terminal and work group ratios can be aggregated at the company level
TERMINAL	Service Failure Frequency Was the pickup or delivery successful?	There should be correlation between performance area ratios – one leads and one lags
WORK GROUP	Dock Service Index Missed Pickups Billing Errors OS&D Exceptions Complaint Calls AR Sales Days Are we anticipating potential failures?	Each process has at least one 'quality' performance area ratio

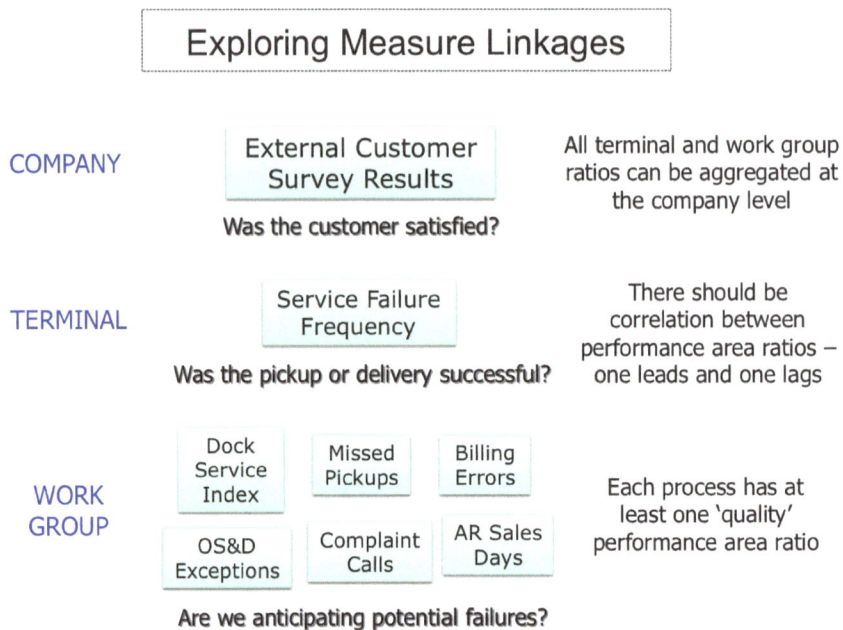

The best way to get started with building balanced scorecards for your work group or organization begins with the completion of a scorecard summary matrix, similar to the example shown on the facing page. If you were simply creating a balanced scorecard for your workgroup, you would only need to complete one row of this matrix (your vital signs). This might seem easy, but selecting the measures themselves for a given scorecard is often where the true measurement system building challenges become evident.

The true power of using this tool comes to light however when a company's, or plant's, leadership team sits down and creates an entire summary matrix. In doing so, they normally define (1) a more complete set of measures for each workgroup, (2) measures for workgroups that may not be using them at all, and (3) the linkages that exist across each performance area.

In performance areas such as safety and people, the measures are often the same. Quality and cost measures however often differ significantly between departments. It is also common to see many departments that currently look only at safety and throughput measures – completing a summary matrix using the common operations performance areas mentioned previously helps ensure that key cost, quality, and people measures are tracked and trended as well.

The best companies use this type of approach to ensure that all workgroups are supporting the strategic goals of the company. This approach also helps link key process performance responsibilities to each process owner in the company, instead of focusing merely on departmental performance that actually reflects a composite set of performance results for several key processes and the actions of multiple leaders. Spending an hour or so to complete this simple matrix can have a profound effect!

On the next two pages, you will find examples of matrices that are used to help organizations see the degree of alignment that exists between their different measures across departments. The first example reflects alignment by key performance area (KPA). The second example reflects alignment against the mission and the five strategic objectives of the organization.

Example Scorecard Summary Matrix

Team	Key Performance Areas and Measures			
	SAFETY	PEOPLE	QUALITY	COST
Plant	# of LT Accidents OSHA Incident Rate	Absenteeism % Turnover % Survey Score	Waste % Rework % Back Order Rate	Cost per Pound Cost per Manhour
Production	# of LT Accidents OSHA Incident Rate	Absenteeism % Turnover %	Waste % Rework % Monthly Inspection Score	Cost per Pound Cost per Manhour Efficiency %
Maintenance	# of LT Accidents OSHA Incident Rate	Absenteeism % Turnover %	Repeat Repairs rate Monthly Inspection Score Internal Customer Sat	Cost per Pound Cost per Manhour Downtime %
Warehouse	# of LT Accidents OSHA Incident Rate	Absenteeism % Turnover %	Back Order Rate Monthly Inspection Score Order Accuracy %	Cost per Pound Cost per Manhour Orders per Manhour
Sanitation	# of LT Accidents OSHA Incident Rate	Absenteeism % Turnover %	Pre-Op Score - average Monthly Inspection Score Internal Customer Sat	Cost per Pound Cost per Manhour
Quality Assurance	# of LT Accidents OSHA Incident Rate	Absenteeism % Turnover %	Internal Customer Sat Complaint Rate	Cost per Pound Cost per Manhour

The term 'balanced scorecard' has been in the business main stream for over twenty-five years now, but not necessarily in a front line, process-focused form. While it is true that the high performing organizations use balanced scorecards across their business units, sites, and processes, many organizations still limit their use to the business unit and site levels. In most cases, balanced scorecards have not been defined for all key processes, and process owners are not looking at daily process performance from a balanced, 'vital signs' perspective.

Balanced scorecards can help you improve in several ways. First, they help you make sure that one performance area is not focused on at the expense of others – that a mission-focus is maintained. Second, they convey a stronger visual message to your people about what is important. Finally, if you convert your scorecard data into charts and graphs, you can gain the benefits of the 'picture is worth a thousand words' saying – you will get better results!

In the above example, a balanced set of measures has been defined for the four key performance areas that are common to most, if not all, operations groups. Completing a summary scorecard matrix similar to this one is the first step you should take in beginning to use balanced scorecards in your own organization or to improve the key processes you are responsible for.

By simply completing this table in a two-hour leadership team meeting, your team will gain a lot of clarity about what is important and gain some insight into why you may not have been improving in each of these areas. Most organizations focus on cost or throughput measures at the expense of safety, morale (people), and quality, whether they will admit it or not. If you don't believe me, ask your people what measures they think management is most interested in.

This table also provides a quick overview of measure use by type – the mix of leading / lagging indicators, and count / ratio mixes, can be easily checked by scanning the table. Reaching leadership consensus on measure type however may prove to be challenging as well.

Example MOM Matrix

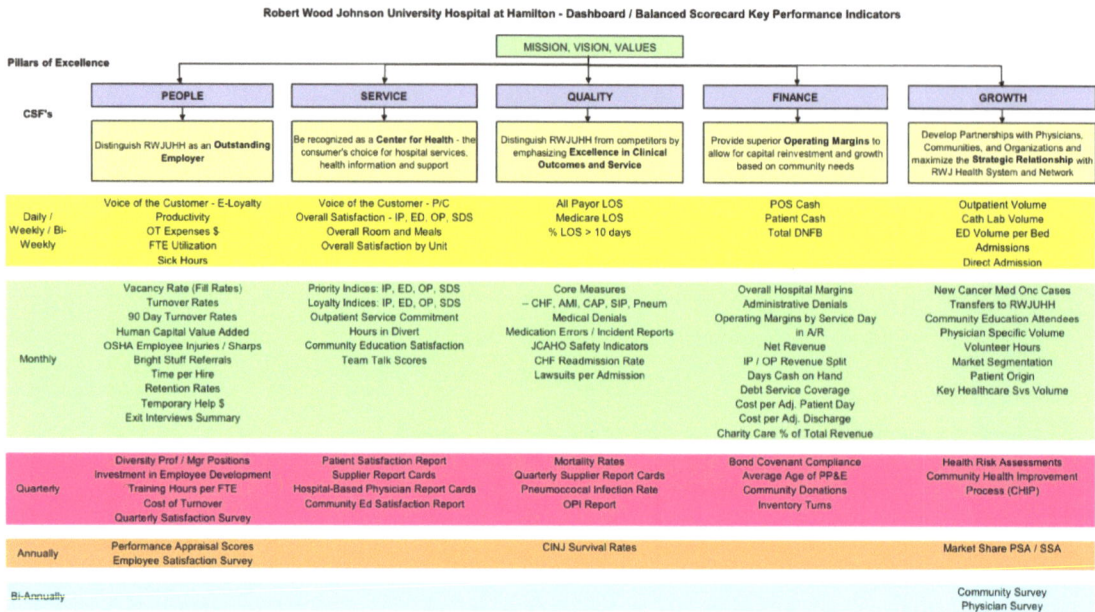

Robert Wood Johnson University Hospital at Hamilton - Dashboard / Balanced Scorecard Key Performance Indicators

	MISSION, VISION, VALUES				
Pillars of Excellence	PEOPLE	SERVICE	QUALITY	FINANCE	GROWTH
CSF's	Distinguish RWJUHH as an **Outstanding Employer**	Be recognized as a **Center for Health** - the consumer's choice for hospital services, health information and support	Distinguish RWJUHH from competitors by emphasizing **Excellence in Clinical Outcomes and Service**	Provide superior **Operating Margins** to allow for capital reinvestment and growth based on community needs	Develop Partnerships with Physicians, Communities, and Organizations and maximize the **Strategic Relationship** with RWJ Health System and Network
Daily / Weekly / Bi-Weekly	Voice of the Customer - E-Loyalty Productivity OT Expenses $ FTE Utilization Sick Hours	Voice of the Customer - P/C Overall Satisfaction - IP, ED, OP, SDS Overall Room and Meals Overall Satisfaction by Unit	All Payor LOS Medicare LOS % LOS > 10 days	POS Cash Patient Cash Total DNFB	Outpatient Volume Cath Lab Volume ED Volume per Bed Admissions Direct Admission
Monthly	Vacancy Rate (Fill Rates) Turnover Rates 90 Day Turnover Rates Human Capital Value Added OSHA Employee Injuries / Sharps Bright Stuff Referrals Time per Hire Retention Rates Temporary Help $ Exit Interviews Summary	Priority Indices: IP, ED, OP, SDS Loyalty Indices: IP, ED, OP, SDS Outpatient Service Commitment Hours in Divert Community Education Satisfaction Team Talk Scores	Core Measures – CHF, AMI, CAP, SIP, Pneum Medical Denials Medication Errors / Incident Reports JCAHO Safety Indicators CHF Readmission Rate Lawsuits per Admission	Overall Hospital Margins Administrative Denials Operating Margins by Service Day in A/R Net Revenue IP / OP Revenue Split Days Cash on Hand Debt Service Coverage Cost per Adj. Patient Day Cost per Adj. Discharge Charity Care % of Total Revenue	New Cancer Med Onc Cases Transfers to RWJUHH Community Education Attendees Physician Specific Volume Volunteer Hours Market Segmentation Patient Origin Key Healthcare Svs Volume
Quarterly	Diversity Prof / Mgr Positions Investment in Employee Development Training Hours per FTE Cost of Turnover Quarterly Satisfaction Survey	Patient Satisfaction Report Supplier Report Cards Hospital-Based Physician Report Cards Community Ed Satisfaction Report	Mortality Rates Quarterly Supplier Report Cards Pneumococcal Infection Rate OPI Report	Bond Covenant Compliance Average Age of PP&E Community Donations Inventory Turns	Health Risk Assessments Community Health Improvement Process (CHIP)
Annually	Performance Appraisal Scores Employee Satisfaction Survey		CINJ Survival Rates		Market Share PSA / SSA
Bi-Annually					Community Survey Physician Survey

SOURCE: Robert Wood Johnson University Hospital at Hamilton Baldrige Application Summary   www.quality.nist.gov

MOM = Mission, Objectives, Measures

The design of the above table, which comes from a past Baldrige award recipient, helps make it easier to reach consensus on a set of measures to use. Five different frequency levels – such as daily, monthly, and quarterly – help people see how different measures are indicators of different types of things. Vertically, the table is designed to show how measures are aligned with the five different strategic focus areas for the organization.

Only select measures in this example have a process focus however. To facilitate that type of measure definition, a chart similar to the one above would need to be created for (1) each process in the value stream and (2) each key value stream support process. This is not that hard to do, but it is often seen as being quite different. Creating a Mission – Objectives – Measures (MOM) matrix at the process level helps further integrate daily activities with the mission and objectives of the team, site, or business unit.

As with the previous example, this table also provides a quick overview of measure use by type – leading / lagging indicator and count / ratio mixes can easily be checked. In general, you want to be able to see the degree that you are:

Using the right MEASURES to measure the right THINGS to make the right CHOICES.

What does the mix of measures you use in your organization say about what is important and what gets rewarded? What measures are trended over time and broken into levels of detail, and which measures are rarely checked? What percentage of your vital signs are not being monitored? Which measures do your people think are the most important to management?

The Role of Operational Definitions

GWS Building Code!

What are they?

- A description of what something is and precisely how it is measured

Why are they necessary?

- Without operational definitions, a specification is meaningless
- Value depends on the method of measure and definition
- Specific criteria will help eliminate standard misinterpretation

Ask yourself the following ...

- Exactly what is to be counted or measured?
- How are the counts or measures taken?
- How much disagreement might exist on this definition?
- Would a reference or set of references be helpful?
- Where is the definition written down?

Deming's Theory of Knowledge tells us that there is no such thing as a true value. The result of any measurement that we make depends on the method used for making it – both how the measure is defined and how it is calculated. Having stated this, you can hopefully see how much misunderstanding is created by the lack of operational definitions. Think of all of the statistical results that you hear of each day, both at work and away from it. How often are formal definitions created for such measures and results prior to them being calculated and used?

For example, consider the census that is taken in the United States every ten years. Think of all of the decisions and changes that hinge on the results of this census. Think also of how that census is taken -- how accurate are the results? Do all of the people who complete the survey have operational definitions to reference as they provide information related to race, income, and age? Does the lack of consistent measure definitions affect the quality of the data?

Another example exists with the opinion polls that are taken prior to political elections. Before a pollster asks a question, does he or she explain the operational definitions of the words that make up the question? While correcting this misunderstanding would be difficult and costly, it does indicate how easily data results can be swayed by the way words are used, spoken, and interpreted. Without operational definitions, data quality will be compromised to some degree.

An operational definition usually has three parts. These parts -- test method, criteria, and decision needed -- are not inherently good or bad. They just represent a system for communicating and measuring. To get agreement in people's minds, we need operational definitions for any specification, standard operating procedure, instruction, measure, or regulation. Operational definitions allow everyone to come to the same conclusion and use the same point of reference. Their meaning is the same today as it is tomorrow.

Great Systems!
"Simple systems, great results!"

Selecting Key Measures

Measure Definition Questions

- Count or ratio?
- Leading or lagging?
- Outcome or in-process?
- Macro or micro?

Ratio Types

- Time-based (clock or people)
- Transaction-based
- Cost-based
- Driver-based

What Determines Frequency?

- Transaction rate / cycle time
- Error or defect?
- Need to learn rate?
- Need to improve rate?

Key Design Questions

- How do we select our measures?
- How do we select our color ranges?
- How do we react to our trends?
- How should we review performance?

Each process scorecard should have 2-3 ratios per KPA

As you consider the different factors associated with measure selection, look over the two examples that were previously provided. The first example is a generic scorecard summary table for a food manufacturing plant. Notice how the measures change, or in some cases like safety, remain the same as you go between work groups within a column. Looking across a given row provides the measures that make up the scorecard for that group or process area.

The second example – the MOM matrix - is more detailed, in that it shows how daily, weekly, monthly, and quarterly measures are linked to both the different departments and the five strategic objectives of the organization. It is a best practice to use your mission, vision, and values to define (1) your strategic objectives and then (2) the key performance areas that are aligned with those objectives.

Measure Definition Questions and Ratio Types

Leading, process-based ratios are the best type of measures to have, but in order to be able to spot that measure type, you need to be familiar with each of the four different measure characteristics (leading, lagging, counts, and ratios). Also, there are four main types of ratios, with percent of total presenting a fifth ratio-based means of measuring.

What Determines Frequency?

Process cycle time is the main determinant, as data is generated with each cycle, and slow cycle processes take longer (less frequent measurement) to collect a good sample size of data. All key errors and defects should be tracked each day. I found that the pain of tracking them served as extra incentive for putting good fixes in place to prevent their reoccurrence.

Key Design Questions

You should be able to define at least a 4 – 5 step process as a response for each of the four Key Design questions shown in the above graphic. Using a defined approach to measurement system design will help ensure consistency across groups.

What are Your Vital Signs?

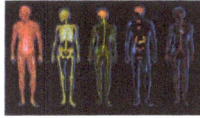

GWS Building Code!

Human Body	Dental Office	Food Plant
• Heartbeats / minute	• Revenue / office hour	• Pounds / minutes
• Blood pressure	• Visits / office hour	• Cost / pound
• Respirations / minute	• Complaints / M visits	• OSHA accident rate
• Body mass index	• OOPs errors / M Visits	• Non-conformance rate
• Years of age	• Staff retention rate	• Retention rate

A process scorecard shows the vital signs for that process (1-2 ratios per KPA)

What are your vital signs? There are a lot of different measures that can be referenced to give you an idea of how well your body is operating, but which measures are the best indicators of body process effectiveness? Which measures can you look at and right away tell if things are going well or not? **Every process has vital signs, even if we have yet to define what they are.** What are the vital signs for the processes you are responsible for?

From a personal health perspective, your vital signs are respiration rate, blood pressure, temperature, and pulse rate. More recently, pain level as been added as a fifth vital sign. If you have made a visit to the doctor lately, even if only for a check-up, it is likely that your vital signs were taken and recorded, just as they had been collected on prior visits.

Believe it or not, vital signs were not captured on a consistent basis until the early 1960s. Now in healthcare, it seem as if there are too many measures in use. From a patient perspective however, it is important to note that the vital signs mentioned above remain as initial diagnostic indicators of a patient's relative health.

Shown above are two additional examples of what a set of vital signs might look like for a dental office or a food plant. I have learned that key indicators of organizational and team health can be developed, just as they have been defined for the human body. *Note that all of the measures are rates in order to help see the relationships between system performance factors.*

It is key to note that all but one of the above examples is stated in the form of RATIOS. Keep in mind that any process count can be converted into a time-based, cost-based, or percentage of total-based ratio. Time and money are spent with each process cycle, which enables the creation of time and cost-based ratios. Classifying counts by type enables the creation of 'percent of total' ratios, and in turn, Pareto charts to help identify high leverage improvement areas as your measures are used to further improve process performance.

Great Systems!
"Simple systems, great results!"

Measures Selection Exercise

Work as a team to select ten key measures for gauging team, department, or site performance

In your 1 – 3 minute report out, cover:

- What ten measures did you pick?

- What process was used to pick them?

  -- What steps, reasons, decision criteria, etc. were used?

- What did you learn and take away from this exercise?

Overview	10 minutes
Small Group Work	45 minutes
Group Report Outs	45 minutes

100 total minutes

Measure ID Card Layout

Leading or Lagging?	Top Ten Measure?	Count or Ratio?
	Performance Measure Name	
Update Frequency?		Who tracks it?

Key Performance Areas

Safety - Green   Cost - Pink   Growth - Orange

People - Blue   Cust. Sat. - Yellow

Measures Selection Exercise Steps

Select 10 key measures which best reflect true process performance

Exercise Process

1. Create 2 x 1 sheet working space on wall w/ flipchart paper

2. Draw Le/La/C/R grid on working space (see page 38)

3. Work as a group to identify possible measures

- One per Post-It – write in center – use assigned KPA color
- Use example layout to complete each measure Post-It

4. Place each completed Measure Post-It in its position on the grid

5. Work as a group to select 10 key measures

6. Prepare a 1-3 minute report out

LAGGING COUNTS	LEADING COUNTS
LAGGING RATIOS	**LEADING RATIOS**

Exploring Possible Safety Measures

	Lagging	**Leading**
Counts	# of recordable accidents # of first aid accidents reported External audit citations or fines Workers Comp costs # of lost work days Cost of lost productivity	# of near misses reported # of tailgate meetings held # of at risk behaviors observed # of findings or repeat findings # of safety training hours # of fixes implemented
Ratios	Lost Time Incident rates Recordable Incident rates External audit citations per year WC costs per employee hour Incident Severity rate Added cost per product made	ARB observations / person # of audit findings / audit Training hours / hours worked # repeat findings / audit Ideas implemented / person Culture assessment percentiles

Exploring Possible Quality Measures

	Lagging	**Leading**
Counts	# of process defects # of rework pounds # of lost customers # of customer returns # of customer complaints # of product recalls	# of audits performed # of findings or repeat findings Hours spent on quality projects # of ideas implemented # of customer touches # of BBQ (human error) catches
Ratios	Defects / 1,000 units made Rework or Waste % Customer retention rate Return $ as % of sales Complaints per day Recalls per year	# of audit findings / audit AFW improvement hours / person # of ideas implemented / person % on improvement teams Positive BBQ catches / person Referrals per customer

Monthly Scorecards

Advantages

→ Stresses measure balance and a systems view

→ Appreciates process capability

→ Provides an index for benchmarking and recognition

→ Helps build a continuous improvement focus

→ Makes daily performance and progress visual

Features

→ Standard format for all workgroups

→ Large white or bulletin board in work area

→ Excel-based version allows easy reporting to others

Personally, I prefer a daily scorecard. Convincing people to create and use monthly scorecards however is tough enough – they think it takes too much time to collect and crunch all of that data. That said, I don't know how process owners can go days without some fact-based means of gauging how well their key processes are performing. Just being there, or using one's gut, are not good enough barometers to me if high performance is one's goal.

While 'too much time' perceptions may, or may not, be supported by fact, they must be appreciated. Scorecards must be fed by lean data capture systems – systems that easily capture the right counts at the process level – the right counts for each process cycle (transaction). If you don't make data capture easy, it won't happen consistently. Ironically, if we captured more daily data, preparing monthly summary reports would not be as challenging.

Scorecards are similar to the sports page in newspapers that lists all of the box scores for each game (each shift is seen as a game). In one look, a person can tell how a process is performing, where its areas of strength and weakness lie, and what types of improvements are planned. Report frequency options will become a non-issue as technology makes it easier to capture data. Selecting and using the right measures will continue to remain a point of challenge, as humans will still be making those decisions.

A one-page scorecard is used at the end of each month to summarize each workgroup's performance (an example is provided in this book). An enlarged version of this scorecard can be displayed in each work area, along with a "whiteboard" graph of day-to-day performance for the key measures in each key performance area. Month-to-month performance trend graphs, complete with control limits, can also be generated from the performance summary spreadsheet, and posted next to these other visual displays. Feedback drives motivation!

If you actually score your monthly scorecard, the YTD scoring summary can be used to show positive or negative trends in total score for the process team as the months go by. The primary objective of this tool is to encourage a balanced look at performance measurement and improvement. By using a balanced scorecard, people are encouraged to look at overall performance over time instead of just the one or two measures that get the most attention.

Weighting and Scoring a Scorecard

Steps

1. Identify key measures
2. Assign weights to each measure
3. Set performance ranges for each
4. Set up work area scoreboard
5. Define measurement procedures
6. Begin using scorecard

Process

1. Track measures daily if possible
2. Complete scorecard at end of each day
3. Share results with all employees
4. Identify improvements to raise score
5. Make adjustments as priorities change

Key Measure	Wt.	Perf. Range	Actual Result	Score
Lost Time Accident Ratio	5	0 to .5 = 10 .6 to 1.0 = 7 1.1 to 1.5 = 5 1.6 to 2.0 = 3 Over 2.0 = 0	.7	35
Terminal Efficiency	4	Over 100% = 10 95 to 100% = 7 90 to 94% = 5 85 to 90% = 3 Under 85% = 0	98%	28
Service Failures per Day	5	0 to 1.0 = 10 1.1 to 2.0 = 7 2.1 to 3.0 = 5 3.1 to 4.0 = 3 Over 4 = 0	2.5	25
Internal Survey -- % Favorable	4	80 or Over = 10 75 to 79 = 7 70 to 74 = 5 65 to 69 = 3 Under 65 = 0	85	40
Date: 10/25/02			Total Score	128

There are several ways to design balance into a scorecard and into a measurement system:

Number and Type of Key Performance Areas – Most organizations have a similar set of key performance areas. In a cost center, these areas are normally safety, service or quality, cost (which includes throughput ratios), and people. In a profit center, a fifth revenue generation performance area is added to reflect the need of certain processes to generate sales revenue. A given performance area can be given more than one slot in the vital signs mix if it strategically makes sense to do so. For example, in our trucking company we had more than one Service metric – the on time delivery % and the freight claims ratio.

Number and Type of Vital Signs – The number and type of vital signs – key process measures – directly affects scorecard balance. A performance area can have more than one key measure if you want to add more weight to that area relative to the others. For example, if you want to emphasize service over efficiency, you can have two service measures, but only one efficiency measure, in your mix of vital signs.

Varying the number and type of measures per key performance area amplifies the overall impact of that area. By reaching consensus on this measure mix, the leadership team also moves closer towards strategic consensus. If possible, use no more than five to seven vital signs per scorecard. Remember, the process team should be able to directly influence each measure – ideally, use process-based counts to create your leading ratio vital signs.

Assign weights to each measure – If you use scoring to link performance to recognition, you will need to assign a weight to each measure. By assigning weight to each key measure, you are using a third approach for awarding more points when a given performance area does well. Values between 1 (low) and 5 (high) are typically used to assign weights. As an example, if you wanted to emphasize service relative to the other measures, you would assign that measure a weight of "5", and give the other measures a weight of "4" or less.

The example shown below should give you a better picture of what a 'points-based' scorecard might look like after it has been set up. This approach is used when a work group or company wants to link some form of formal recognition to the performance of a work group or site.

Monthly Terminal Performance Scorecard -- Portland Terminal

# of LT Accidents	Revenue Growth %	Terminal Efficiency	# of Missed Pickups	# of Late Deliveries	Control. Expense %	Points Poss.
0	Over 11.0	Over 95.5	Under 2	Under 10	Under 40	10
--	11.0	95.5	2	10	40.2	9
--	10.5	95.0	3	15	40.4	8
--	10.0	94.5	4	20	40.6	7
--	9.5	94.0	5	25	40.8	6
1	9.0	93.5	6	30	41.0	5
--	8.5	93.0	7	35	41.2	4
--	8.0	92.5	8	40	41.4	3
--	7.5	92.0	9	45	41.6	2
--	7.0	91.5	10	50	41.8	1
More than 1	Under 7.0	Under 91.5	Over 10	Over 50	Over 41.8	0
1	7.4	94.3	2	45	40.5	Actual
5	2	7	9	2	7	Points
5	4	4	4	4	4	Weight
25	8	28	36	8	28	Score

Total Score for Month = ⬛ 133

This example scorecard has a maximum of 250 possible points per month. Its design places a greater emphasis on service, as there are two service measures, and only one measure for each of the other key performance areas (safety, revenue, efficiency, and costs). The maximum score can only be obtained by first understanding how the measures work together as a system. Attempting to maximize the performance of one or more measures without this understanding will result in poor performances in one or more of the other areas.

Note that in those cases where an actual value did not match up exactly with a value in a performance range, rounding was used to determine how many points to assign. Scorecards, including performance range selection, are set up as part of the annual planning process. Control charts are used to project the probability of obtaining a given number of points in each category – obtaining a high score can be as easy or as difficult as you want it to be.

Goal Setting Process

1. Select process and measure for goal setting
2. Define historical range for baseline average and limits
3. List expected process improvements and timings
4. Identify potential impact for each planned improvement
5. Select goal(s) that matches desired probability of success

The easy way to set goals is to simply expect performance to be some percentage higher than last year's average. Such a goal setting approach ignores process capability and can result in unrealistic performance expectations being set however. The five-step process shown here is recommended as an alternative approach – consider giving it a try!

Two Strategies for Setting Performance Goals

Before you can actually set performance ranges for each key measure, you have select between two possible strategies. The first strategy is to use past performance as a goal setting foundation. The second strategy is based on reaching a desired level of performance.

Past performance strategy -- With this approach, you are trying to improve over the performance for last month, last year, or some other period of time. Historical data, preferably from control charts, is used. Using control chart data helps you estimate the likelihood of certain performance levels being achieved and recognition dollars being spent.

One way to set up a performance range is to begin by matching the historical average with the "5 point" box. The upper and lower control limits are then paired up with the "7" and "3" point boxes. This strategy awards more points for positive fundamental system change, for without such change, more than 7 points will be earned only 15% of the time.

Desired level of performance strategy -- This strategy is used for performance areas like safety or service where a minimum number of "mistakes" is desired, no matter what the system is currently capable of. With this strategy, much more of an improvement effort and focus is required to receive a high number of points. If this strategy is selected for use, those who select it must be willing to support the amount of extra effort required to score well, or frustration will be the end result instead of implemented improvements (zero is tough to obtain and sustain).

Once you have selected a strategy, set up each performance range by first putting in place the process average (5), and high and low control limits. Fill in the gaps by making incremental steps between each point level until you have assigned a performance value to each of the ten points on the scorecard for that measure. Test the usability of your scorecard by scoring one or more previous days, weeks, or months of performance from the past.

Understanding Variation

- Every process has variation

- We want to see variation

- If things appear the same, we aren't close enough to see the difference

- Tolerable amount depends on customer / process impact

- Excess variation wastes money and time

"If I had to reduce my message for management to just a few words, I'd say it all had to do with reducing variation." -- W. Edwards Deming

If we understand a system, we can predict within a range of values how it will perform. This range of performance is known as variation -- the amount of 'bounce' between high and low values for a process when it is measured. All processes have some degree of variation, but this amount can be large or small. If variation is high, it is difficult to provide a consistent product or service, and it is difficult to predict future process performance with any accuracy.

For example, consider the school bus that takes a child from their home to school each day. If we timed the length of this daily trip, we could calculate the average time to make a trip. Most of us know how to do this. What fewer of us recognize is that we could also predict the percent of time the bus would be within two, five, or ten minutes of the average. Understanding the variation in this child delivery system would allow us to make this type of prediction.

Most systems exhibit behavior that is distributed normally. The resultant bell curve shows a typical, and stable, normal distribution. There are some systems that follow a different distribution, such as exponential, but most are "normal." You can use a check sheet, and then a histogram, to explore the variation in some, or all, of your key systems.

Some people get hung up on special, versus common, cause variation. According to Shewhart, who Deming learned from, special cause variation only occurs 1 out of 100 times. If your process control chart is showing a higher rate of special cause variation than this, odds are your control limits are not based on data that is reflective of the current process you are charting. It is much more common to see processes that are much too wide – the limits are too far apart.

Variation also tells you what the odds of obtaining a given goal are if no, or minimal' system changes are made. Calculating the standard deviation for a given measure is the first step in making such a projection. Comparing the standard deviation to the average will tell you how much bounce you have in your process for that measure.

Great Systems!
"Simple systems, great results!"

Setting Goals for Color Ranges

Use of historical data

➡ How many months of data should you use?

➡ How much systems change has occurred over time?

➡ What process is used to make data set adjustments?

Probability of Goal Achievement

➡ What 'green' percent can the recognition budget support?

➡ What are the timelines for expected process improvements?

➡ How do colors serve as performance review triggers?

When a system is normally distributed, certain percentages of its values fall within certain distances from the average. This measure of standard deviation (also known as sigma) is used to describe these distances. In normally distributed systems, 99 to 100% of the values will fall within a process width of six standard deviations (three on one side of the average and three on the other). Completing a control chart for a given process metric will help you learn more about the relationships that exist between process average, process width, and predictability.

A key role of management is being able to predict what a system will do. Once a supervisor or manager can predict what their systems will do, they will also have a better idea of what their systems are capable of. As fundamental system changes are made to improve the system or process, the control charts for the affected measures should reflect the success of those changes – in particular, variation (process width) should decrease.

One common area of failure occurs when customer specifications do not match up with what the system is capable of providing. For example, if an emergency room promises to treat ALL patients within 45 minutes after they arrive at the hospital, the value of 45 minutes should be three standard deviations lower than the process average. If it is not, customer expectations will not be met a certain percentage of the time.

Similarly, if sales promises the customer that a part will have a tolerance of plus or minus one inch, the process width of the system should be no wider than this amount. Most people do not know what their systems are capable of providing, because they have not done the measurement and charting. Instead, they make promises to get business, and hope that others will find a way to meet the expectations of these new customers, and in turn, keep them.

All too often, we fail to consider process variation and its impact on potential goal attainment. People get frustrated trying to hit a goal that has a low probability of being realized just as they get stressed trying to improve a measure they have little control over. Both factors should be considered as color ranges are set – what will be required to consistently obtain a 'green' score? Finally, historical data should be used to test all color range assignments to help gain a better understanding of how likely goal achievement really is.

Three Possible Approaches

Change color as standard deviation narrows

GREEN: < 1 STD of process average

YELLOW: 1 - 1.5 STD of process average

RED: > 2.0 STD of process average

Mean or Average

-1σ $+1\sigma$

60 to 75%
90 to 98%
99 to 100%

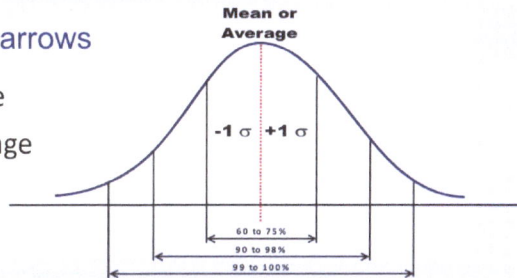

Change color as average improves

GREEN: 5% or more change

YELLOW: Zero to 5% change

RED: Negative change versus average

'Zero-based' Color Change

GREEN: Zero occurrences

YELLOW: 1 occurrence

RED: 2 or more occurrences

Making fair color assignments for any measure requires an understanding of the process or processes that affect that measure. Color assignments should be set based on (1) the expected likelihood of that color being obtained, (2) the need for that color to be obtained, or (3) both factors. *As a measure's data source drifts away from the process level, it becomes less sensitive to individual process shifts and in turn makes it a weaker predictor of process performance.* Aggregated measures also tend to distort variation in one way or another.

Standard deviation reduction colors – This would be the best option to pursue, if only more people knew what it meant. Process variation is managed by reducing process errors, and in turn, increasing process repeatability and consistency. *Processes with lower variation are more predictable, and in turn, better suited to consistently meet or exceed customer expectations.*

'Average improves' colors – This is the more common approach, but its use carries some risk. If an improvement is planned that will drive such a shift, then it makes sense to build such a change into a goal (color assignment). Simply pushing an improvement in average without first defining HOW this improvement will occur can result in more defects reaching the customer, if the process variation is not managed as the primary strategy for improving the process average.

Zero-based colors – This approach for coloring performance areas is based on achieving zero goals – zero incidents, complaints, downtime events, etc. While sustaining, and in some cases even achieving, zero occurrences may be difficult, the strategic importance of a zero focus mandates the use of this measure in some select cases. Historical data should be a fair indicator of 'zero month or day' likelihoods (% of months or days with zero incidents).

When setting goals, consider asking "What factors are we expecting to cause this number to improve?" and "What is the likelihood of this goal being obtained at different locations?"

Great Systems!
"Simple systems, great results!"

Vital Signs, Scorecards, and Goals

Scorecard Setup Exercise -- Setting Performance Monitoring Ranges

The two most common types of scorecard performance ranges are based on either (1) absolute performance goals or on (2) continuous improvement performance goals. Use the examples that have been provided to help you gain a better understanding of how scorecard performance ranges are set up in these two cases.

Absolute Performance Goal -- Lost Time Accident Reduction

Month	# of Accidents
Jan	1
Feb	2
Mar	0
Apr	1
May	1
Jun	3
Jul	1
Aug	0
Sep	0
Oct	2
Nov	1
Dec	2
AVG	1.2
STD	0.9

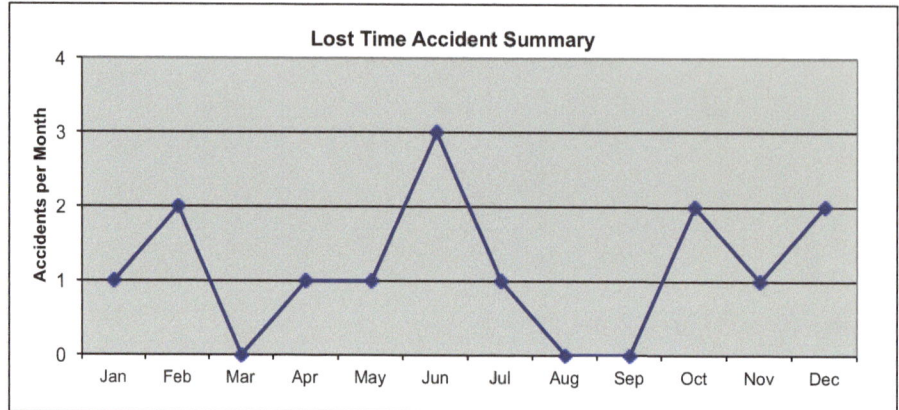

Lost Time Accident Summary

Points	0	1	2	3	4	5	6	7	8	9	10
Color											
Accidents											

HINT: Begin by setting the '0' and '10' point (Red and Green) levels - how many customers can I lose and still get a 'Green' score?

Continuous Improvement Goal -- Defect Reduction

Month	# of Defects	Range
Jan	75	
Feb	63	12
Mar	98	35
Apr	120	22
May	110	10
Jun	75	35
Jul	95	20
Aug	88	7
Sep	110	22
Oct	72	38
Nov	87	15
Dec	75	12
AVG	89	21
STD	17.9	

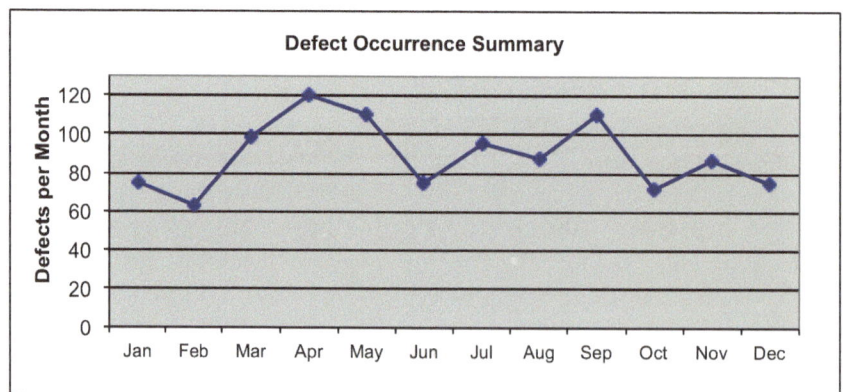

Defect Occurrence Summary

UCL = 144.1   LCL = 33.9

Points	0	1	2	3	4	5	6	7	8	9	10
Color											
Defects											

HINT: Consider the probability of attaining a given # of defects when assigning points and colors

Scorecard Setup Exercise -- Setting Performance Monitoring Ranges

These two exercises illustrate examples where it becomes a little more difficult to set performance ranges. In both cases, performance is improving, but there is still enough variation in the system to cause concern if the goals that are set appear to be too challenging. Remember, system changes should be required to get a high score!

Absolute Performance Goal -- Customer Loss

Month	# of Lost Cust.
Jan	3
Feb	5
Mar	2
Apr	1
May	4
Jun	4
Jul	3
Aug	2
Sep	3
Oct	2
Nov	1
Dec	2
AVG	2.7
STD	1.2

Lost Customers Summary

Points	0	1	2	3	4	5	6	7	8	9	10
Color											
# Lost											

HINT: Begin by setting the '0' and '10' point (Red and Green) levels - how many customers can I lose and still get a 'Green' score?

Continuous Improvement Goal -- Operations Efficiency

Month	Efficiency	Range
Jan	87	
Feb	92	5
Mar	93	1
Apr	94	1
May	90	4
Jun	91	1
Jul	91	0
Aug	96	5
Sep	99	3
Oct	97	2
Nov	95	2
Dec	97	2
AVG	94	2
STD	3.5	

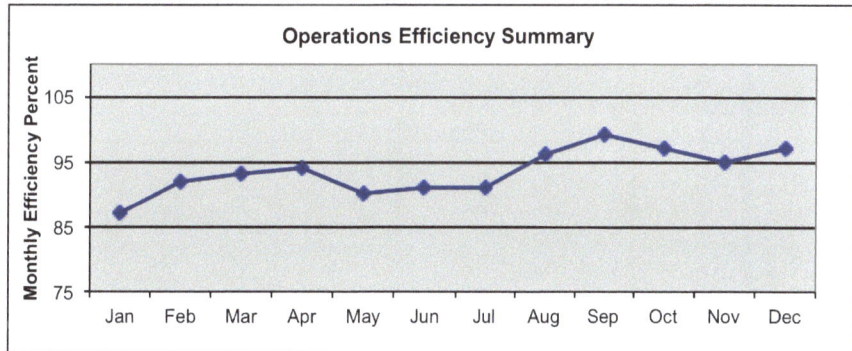

Operations Efficiency Summary

UCL = 99.8   LCL = 87.2

Points	0	1	2	3	4	5	6	7	8	9	10
Color											
Effy %											

HINT: Consider the probability of attaining a given monthly efficiency % when assigning points and colors

Great Systems!
"Simple systems, great results!"

Setting Up a Monthly Scorecard

Performance Area	Weight	Key Performance Measures	Current Average / Process Goal
Safety			
Quality			
People			
Cost			

Setting Up a Balanced Scorecard for a Person, Process, or Outcome
Total Time: 65 minutes

Objective: Identify the key measures, errors, and defects that should be tracked on a daily basis to monitor key process performance, and begin setting up your daily performance scorecard.

Key Questions:
1. What are your team's key performance areas?
2. What measures should be part of your team's daily scorecard?
3. What would your daily performance dashboard look like?

Group Tasks:

1 minute	1. Select roles for the table: scribe / facilitator, timekeeper, reporter.
19 minutes	2. Create an example month-to-date scorecard that might be used to provide process feedback to your teams on a regular basis. As you set up your scorecard, be sure to include at least one measure for each of the four key performance areas (safety, quality, people, and cost).
20 minutes	3. Create an example daily dashboard report that you might use to provide process feedback to your teams on the previous day's performance results. As you set up your dashboard, be sure to include a report section for each of the four key performance areas (safety, quality, people, and cost).

Team Report: 3 minutes per team for doing your report out and 10 minutes for the follow-up large group discussion. *25 total minutes*

As part of the report out, your team should provide an overview of (1) the key features of the month-to-date scorecard and (2) the types of errors, defects, and other information that you might capture in each report section in your example daily dashboard.

Example Month-to-Date Scorecard

Performance Area	Weight	Key Performance Measures	Month-to-Date Results	Score
Safety	5	# of Lost Time Accidents # of Reportable Accidents	0 lost time accidents 2 reportable accidents	
Quality	5	# of non-conformance events # of customer complaints	5 non-conformances 4 customer complaints	
People	4	# of absences and tardies Internal satisfaction score	3 absences + 5 tardies 65% satisfaction score	
Cost	4	Labor cost per unit handled Rework cost per unit handled	$.35 per unit labor cost $.05 per unit rework cost	

Great Systems!
"Simple systems, great results!"

NOTES:

Use It!

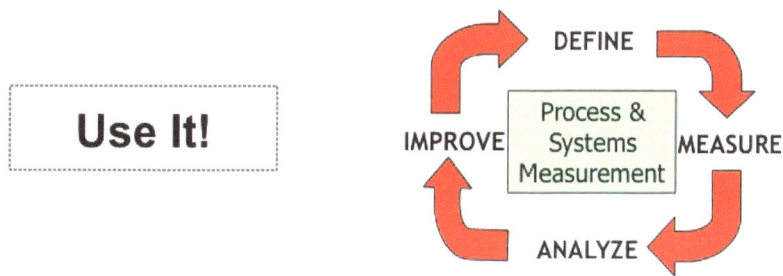

Using Measures to Find Problems and Gauge Progress

- Track key counts and errors, and update database daily
- Use formal approaches to regularly share results
- Consistently recognize efforts to sustain great performance

Meaningful measures are needed as a key ingredient for sustained success. Process teams are often challenged to impact departmental or company performance measures that are somewhat, or largely, beyond their sphere of control (their circle of influence). When this happens, people become frustrated, as they are being held accountable for measures that they only indirectly influence. In addition to getting frustrated, they might also look for ways to beat the system in order to stay out of trouble – by distorting the data, for example.

There are three keys to obtaining "meaningful measures." First, make sure that at least one key measure is established for each key performance area, at each layer of the company. Second, use a summary matrix to make sure that linkage and alignment between measures is maintained within each key focus area for all workgroups. Third, only use base inputs (counts) for those measures that are within the "circle of influence" of each process team.

Empowering each team to make the decisions necessary for improvement serves as the system driver. It makes little sense to charge a team with the responsibility of controlling their costs or accident rate, and not give them the authority to make decisions that would improve their work system in these areas. These teams need to be able to take immediate action!

Include a cost component in each scorecard to help tie the entire system together. In many organizations, front line employees are unaware of (1) the degree to which their daily job impacts the company's financial performance and (2) how significant their daily expenses, including waste, are in general. Your initial goal here should be to simply show each team member how much cost they can personally influence each day.

If you ask the question "Why are we using these measures?", the answer your people give you should be consistent . Answers such as "to better understand a process", "to track our rate of improvement", and "to more quickly spot our key problems" are three key answers you should hope to hear. "Because my boss told me to" is not a good answer.

How Should You Use Your Data?

Commonly stated approaches for using data:

- Review performance
- Find the root cause of problems
- Prioritize improvement efforts
- Set future performance goals
- Recognize and compensate
- Predict future performance

Capture

Error
Reduction
Process

Change

Crunch

**How effectively do you
spend time using data?**

Review performance – Most companies review performance on a monthly basis. Unfortunately, comparisons to budget typically serve as the primary performance analysis tool. Worse yet, these reports are typically made up of only numbers on paper – trends lines for observing performance over time are rarely used. The better practice approach is to use process-based ratios as the primary analysis tool, with year over year, or month over month, trend lines being used to more effectively observe process behavior over time.

Find the root cause of problems – Measuring the right things at a process level will help you better evaluate the effectiveness of different systems that are intended to prevent human error and equipment problems. Using opinion to find root causes will result in fixes that fail.

Prioritize improvements – Risk assessment and multi-voting are two common techniques that used to prioritize improvements. Unfortunately, opinion (instead of facts) often serves as the main reference for deciding which possible improvements are selected or what the impact of a given change on risk levels will be. Multiple decision-making tools, such as Kepner-Tregoe Decision Analysis, exist that allow quantitative factors to be considered as options are evaluated. At a minimum, try to use a decision matrix of some type.

Set future performance goals – Don't make the mistake of simply bumping up last year's average by five or ten percent to set your new performance goals. Instead, use process-based trends to evaluate recent performance levels. Also, as new goals are set, consider the possible impact of expected process changes and improvements that are planned. Additionally, use control limits and variation analysis to determine the probability of actually achieving each goal.

Recognize and compensate – Most organizations base their formal recognition and compensation systems on numbers. The problem is that they often use the wrong numbers in setting recognition levels and compensation hurdles. Recognition and compensation expectations should be based on process vital signs that the person can control by the manner in which they do their job each day, not primarily on actions others are expected to take.

Predict future performance – This is the ultimate reason for using data. If you use the right ratios, in the proper mix, to consistently evaluate process performance, you will be in a much better position to also predict future performance. If you can integrate the use of control limits into your trend charts, you can actually predict the probability of achieving possible goals or more effectively meeting customer needs.

64

Key Process Deployment Tools

Personal Performance Journals

Performance Summary Database

Workplace Scorecards

Workgroup Review Meetings

The steps for implementing this process are simple, but each one is critical. Should you try to put this process in place yourself, you will find it tempting to shortcut one or more steps, or even skip them all together. Doing so will compromise the effectiveness of the measurement system, and most process teams will recognize this fact. Before we look at the implementation steps themselves, let's take an introductory look at the four key tools that are part of process-based measurement.

Four key tools are used to put this process in place – personal performance journals, performance summary databases, monthly scorecards, and workgroup review meetings. These tools are described and illustrated on the next few pages of the book. Keep in mind that these tools can be manual in nature (filling out forms by hand) or digital (data is captured on a tablet, by voice, or via a keyboard). You want to strive for lean data capture, but you don't want the data collection to become so automatic that you lose touch with the daily process.

Personal Performance Journals – In general, a person would complete a one-page journal entry each day relative to the processes they own. Specifically, this form is used to capture key process counts, machine-calculated ratios, and key process problems.

Performance Summary Database – All of the count, ratio, and key problem information from the personal performance journal is captured daily in either a spreadsheet or a database software package. Capturing key daily counts, ratios, and problems in a database allows you to do summary analysis (crunch) the data you have captured for subsequent use.

Workplace Scorecards – Ideally, an updated, color coded scorecard should be posted as each shift is completed. People like to know how they are doing, and daily reports help keep a more consistent emphasis on successes, problems, and vital signs than monthly reports do.

Workgroup Review Meetings – These meetings are used to review key results, and more importantly, to identify improvements that need to be made. Workgroup review meetings offer perhaps the best forum for really using the data that you are capturing and crunching.

Great Systems!
"Simple systems, great results!"

Personal Performance Journals

Advantages

→ Captures daily error and defect event information

→ Helps support and show the benefits of trend analysis

→ Indicates areas where improvement is needed

→ Makes idea capturing and sharing easy

→ Supports problem solving efforts

Questions

→ How will you capture key daily data – iPad or notepad?

→ Who will be required to complete a journal each day?

→ What would some example journal pages look like?

Personal Performance Journals

At the individual level, it is critical that you create a simple system that captures (1) the key ways in which each employee spends their time each day and (2) the key base data inputs for these activities. To accomplish this, each process leader, and in some cases each work team member, should be asked to capture base data on their "Monthly Personal Performance Journal" form (paper-based or spreadsheet) each day. The daily entries in this journal capture the frequency of events that require significant time investment. If possible, provide your people with data from your mainframe computer system whenever possible to minimize the amount of additional data that each person has to manually track.

For example, a customer service representative would track the number of hours they work, the number of problem calls they answer, and the number of information calls they process. A billing clerk would track the number of bills they enter, the total number of billing hours they work, and the total hours they work overall. An assembly line worker might track total hours worked, total pieces produced, and total rework or rejects detected.

On a regular basis (daily is preferred), the process owner will collect the individual forms and summarize the team's data, either on a second form or in a spreadsheet. This summary data would then be captured as a row of data in a performance summary spreadsheet.

Almost daily progress is being made relative to developing tablet-based applications for capturing key process counts, ratios, and problems on a real-time basis. Such systems are more efficient than a manually completed form, simply because the information does not have to be captured twice (once on the form and once in the database). In many cases, this data can also be crunched on a real time basis to provide even better decision-making information.

There is a caution to be aware of however should you choose to go the digital route – automatically capturing the data creates a degree of disconnect between daily process performance and the process owner. If this disconnect becomes too great, people will become less sensitive to problems, and in turn, may begin to accept problems as being normal or "just the way things work around here." There is value associated with manually capturing data daily.

66

Example Personal Performance Journal

Process : _____   Process Owner: _____

Date	Hours Worked	Calls Taken	Problem Calls	Info Calls	Dropped Calls	% in 5 seconds
1	8.0	170	34	136	7	81
2	8.2	162	25	137	8	92
3	8.0	173	20	153	3	73
4	7.9	168	22	146	6	77
5	8.0	180	35	145	2	81
8	8.0	168	28	140	8	78
9	9.0	179	32	147	10	89
10	8.3	150	31	119	7	82
11	8.0	155	21	134	11	71
12	7.8	164	32	132	6	80
15	8.0	159	25	134	3	75
16	8.0	171	36	135	6	76
17	7.8	165	20	145	5	87
18	8.8	156	28	128	10	68
19	8.2	169	33	136	9	72
22	8.0	145	30	115	2	81
23	8.0	159	20	139	4	77
24	8.1	166	21	145	6	84
25	8.0	161	19	142	8	90
26	7.5	170	26	144	6	84
29	8.0	149	29	120	7	88
30	8.2	175	20	155	5	80
31	8.0	165	11	154	3	74
Totals	185.8	3,779	598	3,181	142	1,840

Month: _____

Customer Requirements and Measures

* 80% answered < 5 seconds * Own the call
* Seek first to understand * > 20 calls per hour
*< 5% dropped calls *> 85% information calls

Great Systems!
"Simple systems, great results!"

Performance Summary Database

Advantages

→ Provides daily performance feedback
→ Keeps the user in touch with their processes
→ Captures transaction data for later analysis
→ Makes graph creation much easier
→ Allows for scenario analysis

Features

→ Can set up in Excel, Filemaker, Access, Numbers, etc.
→ Contains base data and performance ratios
→ Also includes monthly and YTD tables, and trend charts

By focusing only on key measures and the base data associated with them, each process owner ends up making an average of five to ten daily data entries into the spreadsheet. Spreadsheets should be set up for each work group to capture these entries, calculate the performance ratios, and update graphs that are included to provide visual feedback to the team. This reporting and spreadsheet updating process is repeated upwards through the organization. Certain key data is taken from each report and added to data that the "next level" team leader is capturing. With today's technology, rolling up process-level data to a site or business unit level is relatively easy.

It is critical that you require EACH process owner, from top to bottom in the organization, to track the performance of those processes that they are responsible for on a daily basis if you want this approach to really work. Additionally, your chances of sustained success will be significantly heightened if you (1) require each process owner to distribute or post their results and (2) review their results with their team and the person they report to at the end of each monthly reporting period. These practices help drive personal accountability and send a strong and consistent message to all process owners about what is important to the organization.

While spreadsheets are much faster at "crunching numbers", you may have several people that need consistent encouragement to get them to use this tool for the first few months of the change effort. To ease the transition, you can simplify the process by creating their initial performance summary spreadsheet for them. Their initial learning goals would in turn involve only opening the spreadsheet, entering data, saving the spreadsheet, and printing their work.

One key advantage of using a spreadsheet can be found in its ability to generate graphs, or pictures, of the daily processes each employee is involved with. Just as it may be a struggle to get some supervisors to crunch numbers in a spreadsheet, it may also be tough at first to get them to use the graphs that are built into them. Because graphs were much too time consuming to create prior to spreadsheets, supervisors in the past simply weren't using them.

Spreadsheets are just one type of database software that can be used. Filemaker, Access, and other packages can also be used for this purpose. The key is to capture the data in a manner that allows trend lines, control charts, and Pareto charts to be created, helping to highlight areas of improvement and areas where additional attention is needed.

Example Performance Summary Spreadsheet - Production Process

Date	Labor Hours	Pounds Produced	Labor Cost	Waste Pounds	Rework Pounds	Pounds/ Hour	Waste %	Rework %	Cost / Pound	Absent or Tardy	Reported Accidents
1	80.5	24,120	$1,235	30	2,100	299.6	0.1%	8.0%	$0.051	1	0
2	82.0	23,546	1,265	1,054	2,204	287.1	3.9%	8.2%	0.054	0	0
3	83.4	24,652	1,293	368	1,983	295.6	1.4%	7.3%	0.052	0	0
4	79.1	23,471	1,207	259	2,142	296.7	1.0%	8.3%	0.051	0	0
5	84.2	23,587	1,309	1,673	2,083	280.1	6.1%	7.6%	0.055	0	1
8	78.6	23,342	1,197	238	1,985	297.0	0.9%	7.8%	0.051	0	0
9	82.1	24,109	1,267	521	1,803	293.7	2.0%	6.8%	0.053	2	0
10	81.3	23,981	1,251	409	2,004	295.0	1.5%	7.6%	0.052	1	0
11	80.9	23,687	1,243	583	2,105	292.8	2.2%	8.0%	0.052	0	0
12	77.8	23,105	1,181	235	2,234	297.0	0.9%	8.7%	0.051	0	0
15	82.7	24,111	1,279	699	1,993	291.5	2.6%	7.4%	0.053	0	0
16	81.3	24,007	1,251	383	2,054	295.3	1.4%	7.8%	0.052	0	0
17	85.3	23,187	1,331	2,403	2,103	271.8	8.7%	7.6%	0.057	0	0
18	81.1	23,678	1,247	652	2,204	292.0	2.5%	8.3%	0.053	0	0
19	82.0	24,321	1,265	279	2,106	296.6	1.0%	7.9%	0.052	0	0
22	80.8	24,187	1,241	53	2,065	299.3	0.2%	7.9%	0.051	1	0
23	79.8	23,921	1,221	19	1,994	299.8	0.1%	7.7%	0.051	1	0
24	81.2	23,899	1,249	461	1,893	294.3	1.8%	7.2%	0.052	0	0
25	82.4	24,001	1,273	719	1,914	291.3	2.7%	7.2%	0.053	0	0
26	77.6	23,110	1,177	170	2,048	297.8	0.7%	8.1%	0.051	0	0
29	80.7	23,143	1,239	1,067	2,098	286.8	4.1%	8.0%	0.054	0	0
30	81.8	24,211	1,261	329	2,107	296.0	1.2%	7.9%	0.052	0	1
31	80.3	23,546	1,231	544	2,148	293.2	2.1%	8.2%	0.052	1	0
Totals	1,866.9	546,922	$28,713	13,148	47,370	293.0	2.2%	7.8%	0.052	7	2

Company Summary Spreadsheet — COUNTS

	Jan	Feb	Mar	Apr	May	Jun	Jul	Aug	Sep	Oct	Nov	Dec	AVG
BASE													
# of working days	20	21	23	22	20	21	21	23	20	22	19	21	21.1
Headcount	45	45	47	50	45	47	48	46	46	45	44	46	46.2
Batches	227	211	350	343	372	367	329	315	257	363	323	376	319.4
Flavors	111	88	170	161	167	199	173	178	129	178	173	194	160.1
SAFETY													
Lost Time Accidents	0	0	0	0	0	0	1	0	0	0	1	0	0.2
Other OSHA Accidents	1	0	0	2	0	1	0	0	2	0	0	0	0.5
First Aid Accidents	5	3	3	2	4	1	3	2	1	1	0	0	2.1
Near Misses Reported	13	18	22	23	25	20	19	17	22	15	18	24	19.7
COST													
Bottles	363,948	352,013	586,484	526,675	506,086	544,198	514,854	469,330	402,330	545,391	482,878	567,382	488,464
Cases	27,896	27,123	43,318	40,220	41,756	43,309	41,132	40,155	30,630	42,649	42,590	46,086	38,905
Pounds Produced	873,475	846,557	1,397,048	1,275,069	1,224,986	1,299,867	1,235,678	1,126,932	967,335	1,307,846	1,157,867	1,361,717	1,172,865
Labor Hours	7,688	11,231	8,682	9,921	10,610	11,702	10,448	11,256	10,025	10,540	9,989	10,428	10,210
Line Hours	165	210	187	176	166	187	175	221	191	199	181	210	189.0
Downtime Hours	16.4	25.1	17.7	18.3	17.4	19.3	18.4	25.3	22.0	21.9	19.1	21.7	20.2
Labor Cost	107,865	121,899	126,686	117,876	126,936	125,274	120,541	117,691	118,171	122,119	123,345	141,861	122,522
QUALITY													
Rework Pounds	87,348	82,345	125,765	122,345	121,211	131,998	124,521	111,766	97,345	128,543	116,334	137,423	115,579
Waste Pounds	8,465	8,573	12,333	11,857	12,155	14,032	12,543	12,021	9,811	13,112	11,564	13,543	11,667
Hold Batches	21	19	23	31	36	34	29	28	22	33	29	36	28.4
Audit Score	85	86	84	88	88	90	91	92	90	89	92	88	88.6
Total Defects	1,343	1,435	2,456	3,422	2,887	2,687	2,511	2,498	1,998	2,776	2,409	2,571	2,416
PEOPLE													
Absences	5	4	4	6	3	2	2	3	5	3	2	1	3.3
Tardies	7	7	8	3	6	5	7	4	4	6	7	4	5.7
Complaints	11	18	5	5	3	16	12	11	9	5	7	3	8.8
Hires	0	0	2	6	0	2	3	0	0	0	4	2	1.6
Quits	0	0	0	3	5	0	2	2	0	1	5	0	1.5

If each process owner is required to improve those processes that he or she is responsible for, a tool similar to the example shown above will need to be used. The content of this table is driven by the daily use of the performance summary spreadsheet. I used the above example on a monthly basis to monitor the number of process transactions that were completed in a given month, the cost of those transactions, and other key inputs and ratios that were associated with their execution. For reference, quarterly summaries are too insensitive on their own to identify problem areas – quarterly and annual summaries are better for gauging progress over time.

Because this data is captured in table form in a spreadsheet, it can easily be trended and analyzed further. Charts can be constructed both for individual input or ratio trends, or to examine relationships that may exist between different numbers (such as rework and throughput rates). The goal of using this tool is to capture all of the key inputs associated with the execution of one or more process cycles, and then link that information to the related costs, defects and errors, and other output results. Once you have collected the inputs, you can create a variety of time-based, and cost-based, ratios that can help you better evaluate process performance over time.

One of the mistakes we make in organizations relates to combining data from different processes together into one big number. This is what we do, for example, when we attempt to control labor costs by only looking at cost center performance to budget on a monthly basis. When we are under budget, we relax. When we are over budget, we try to come up reasons why we are in this position, and we ask people to do a better job at controlling their costs. Unfortunately, we are often looking at the performance of several processes when we evaluate our costs in this manner, and in turn, we are mixing good process performance with bad performances. We are not our focusing limited resources on the areas that really need them.

Because the processes are mixed, it is very difficult to target those processes that need our attention the most, or to recognize those people whose processes improved in the most recent month. How do you analyze process performance? How do you really know what is going on?

Company Summary Spreadsheet   RATIOS

| YTD Performance Counts and Ratios - Go Fast Foods | | | | | | | | | | | | | RATIOS |
	Jan	Feb	Mar	Apr	May	Jun	Jul	Aug	Sep	Oct	Nov	Dec	AVG
BASE													
Batches per day	11	10	15	16	19	17	16	14	13	17	17	18	15.2
Flavors per day	6	4	7	7	8	9	8	8	6	8	9	9	7.6
Bottles per day	18,197	16,763	25,499	23,940	25,304	25,914	24,517	20,406	20,117	24,791	25,415	27,018	23,168
Pounds per day	43,674	40,312	60,741	57,958	61,249	61,898	58,842	46,997	48,367	59,448	60,940	64,844	55,630
SAFETY													
LTA Rate	0.0	0.0	0.0	0.0	0.0	0.0	19.1	0.0	0.0	0.0	20.0	0.0	3.3
Other OSHA Rate	26.0	0.0	0.0	40.3	0.0	17.1	0.0	0.0	39.9	0.0	0.0	0.0	9.8
First Aid Rate	130.1	53.4	69.1	40.3	75.4	17.1	57.4	35.5	20.0	19.0	0.0	0.0	40.8
Near Misses per day	0.7	0.9	1.0	1.0	1.3	1.0	0.9	0.7	1.1	0.7	0.9	1.1	0.9
COST													
Labor Cost per Bottle	0.296	0.346	0.216	0.224	0.251	0.230	0.234	0.251	0.294	0.224	0.255	0.250	0.251
Labor Cost per Case	3.867	4.494	2.925	2.931	3.040	2.893	2.931	2.931	3.858	2.863	2.896	3.078	3.149
Labor Cost per Pound	0.123	0.144	0.091	0.092	0.104	0.096	0.098	0.104	0.122	0.093	0.107	0.104	0.104
Daily Hours per Person	8.5	11.9	8.0	9.0	11.8	11.9	10.4	10.6	10.9	10.6	11.9	10.8	10.5
Line Hours per Day	8.3	10.0	8.1	8.0	8.3	8.9	8.3	9.6	9.6	9.0	9.5	10.0	9.0
Bottles per Line Minute	36.8	27.9	52.3	49.9	50.8	48.5	49.0	35.4	35.1	45.7	44.5	45.0	43.1
Overtime %	6.8%	48.6%	0.4%	12.7%	47.4%	48.2%	29.6%	33.0%	36.2%	33.1%	49.4%	34.9%	31.1%
Downtime %	9.9%	12.0%	9.5%	10.4%	10.5%	10.3%	10.5%	11.4%	11.5%	11.0%	10.6%	10.3%	10.7%
Labor Cost / Labor Hour	14.03	10.85	14.59	11.88	11.96	10.71	11.54	10.46	11.79	11.59	12.35	13.60	12.00
QUALITY													
Rework %	9.1%	8.9%	8.3%	8.8%	9.0%	9.2%	9.2%	9.0%	9.1%	8.9%	9.1%	9.2%	9.0%
Waste %	1.0%	1.0%	0.9%	0.9%	1.0%	1.1%	1.1%	1.0%	1.1%	1.0%	1.0%	1.0%	1.0%
Hold Batch %	9.3%	9.0%	6.6%	9.0%	9.7%	9.3%	8.8%	8.9%	8.6%	9.1%	9.0%	9.6%	8.9%
Findings per Audit	25	22	18	23	25	14	12	13	16	19	12	20	18.3
Defects per M Bottles	3.7	4.1	4.2	6.5	5.7	4.9	4.9	5.3	5.0	5.1	5.0	4.5	4.9
PEOPLE													
Absenteeism %	0.6%	0.4%	0.4%	0.5%	0.3%	0.2%	0.2%	0.3%	0.5%	0.3%	0.2%	0.1%	0.3%
Tardy %	0.8%	0.7%	0.7%	0.3%	0.7%	0.5%	0.7%	0.4%	0.4%	0.6%	0.8%	0.4%	0.6%
Turnover Rate	0.0%	0.0%	0.0%	6.0%	11.1%	0.0%	4.2%	4.3%	0.0%	2.2%	11.4%	0.0%	3.2%
Complaint %	1.2%	1.9%	0.5%	0.5%	0.3%	1.6%	1.2%	1.0%	1.0%	0.5%	0.8%	0.3%	0.9%

When I was the plant manager at a food plant, these were the minimum mix of counts and ratios I would capture every month. Most process owners can come up with a similar set of tables for their own processes if they (1) begin by defining key counts for each key performance area and then (2) define ratios that are based on using those counts.

I can't express strongly enough how important it is to capture key counts and ratios daily. On more than one occasion, I have had to try to go back in time and re-capture old data. This is not easy to do to begin with, and some really big questions about data integrity are sure to arise even if you can find the data. If you can't capture key counts daily, or if you are working with long cycle processes that don't have daily cycles, the monthly tables like those shown on this page and the facing page may work better. Monthly tables (data capture) should be seen as the minimum however – quarterly data rarely provides enough continuity over time to effectively observe real process behavior, and they are not sensitive to process-specific changes.

You will also find that by capturing a variety of key counts for each key performance area, you actually come up with new ratios and new types of correlation analysis simply because you have more numbers to work with. Even though some ratios may already be in use, they may not be as sensitive as you would like, or they may be of a lagging (as opposed to leading) nature. Typically, I tend to capture and crunch more data than I actually use – **the key is to capture enough different types of data to really help you understand the processes you own**.

Also note that some ratios are captured automatically and might need to be treated more like counts (percent of total and chemical ratios come to mind). Ratios are better than counts simply because they show the relationship between two things. Ratios can't be calculated however without first having the counts, and most counts can be converted into time, cost, or percentage ratios if you know how much time or money was spent in obtaining a given count.

Finally, use the power of spreadsheets to create graphs of your captured information. It is tempting to think that you can get the same insights from numbers versus charts, but the human brain does not seem to work that way. A graph, like a picture, is worth a thousand words.

Great Systems!
"Simple systems, great results!"

> ### Work Group Review Meetings
>
> #### Advantages
> → Opportunity to review goals and expectations
>
> → Forum for sharing improvement ideas
>
> → Place to provide feedback and recognition
>
> → Helps build a continuous improvement focus
>
> → Chance to teach and learn from each other
>
> #### Features
> → Meeting frequency and length vary with scope of work
>
> → Two way communication should be encouraged
>
> → Not a forum for formal problem solving

Workgroup Review Meetings

Each workgroup should meet regularly (at least monthly) to review current performance trends in their area of focus. In these meetings, they identify factors that significantly impacted recent performance either positively or negatively, and possible improvements that can be made to improve that performance. Sufficient time is not available in these meetings however to use them as a forum for formal problem solving. Certain team members should participate on formal problem solving / project teams for those problems that require such an effort.

In order to use the scorecard effectively in work group meetings, the following tips are offered:

- Focus on (1) observing the trends that occurred during the most recent month and over the year to-date, (2) discussing possible theories for these trends, and (3) identifying possible corrective actions that can be taken to improve performance. Try to match recent system changes to graphical shifts in performance to help validate the effectiveness of recent improvements.

- Look for relationships between measures, similar to the efficiency – service tradeoff that was presented earlier. Use simple behavior (control) charts to define possible theories, and use quality tools such as Pareto charts and scatter diagrams to explore these theories with further data analysis.

- Ensure that a process for capturing and channeling possible improvement ideas exists. While workgroups don't have the time for formal problem solving, they are your best source for improvement ideas. Ask each process owner to maintain a key project list for this purpose. Also, let your people know that they can add an idea to that list at any time.

- Training people how to use the different measurement system tools is also key. This training can be provided in a supervisor skills workshop, through computer-based training, and through one-to-one support. Your program may be coordinated by one person, but all upper managers, including the people "at the top", should have the responsibility of ensuring that the people who report to them understand the process, and use these tools properly and consistently to help them do so.

- It should be stressed that using the data as a hammer will only result in inaccurate information, and that blame should be placed on the system instead of on the individual. You should also emphasize that each leader's scorecard will contain a measurement for internal customer satisfaction, and that incorrect data use could result in a lower than desired satisfaction survey score.

Example Daily Dashboard

Daily Syrup Production Summary   021

				Volume:			Productivity		
							$/case	$/bottle	Hrs/Th
Date:	21-Jan-04	Prod:	750 P	7,252	bottles	959.8 cases	0.51	0.068	36.7
Shift	Days		750 G	38,068	bottles	3,299.8 cases	0.50	0.043	36.3
Supervisor	Kevin		50 ml	2,000	bottles	16.7 cases	43.28	0.361	2418.0
			.5 G Sauce	5,400	jugs	900.0 cases	0.57	0.095	42.4
			Rework	2,160	bottles	180.0 cases	1.15	0.096	81.1

966 Borders / WM Six Packs   1 int'l batch - GER (1)

Lost Time: Case Coder -- 5 min used to adjust case coder print quality -- 021404
Changeover -- 46 min used to change from 750 P to 750 G
Batching -- 24 min lost due to high brix batch / no test before transfer

Safety: No injuries
0 on light duty
0 out on injury

Other Costs: $118 - Make Borders six packs

Quality: Hold -- One batch of 750 GER Vanilla for high brix -- 021435
Hold -- 367 cases of 750 SF Vanilla for suspect pH -- 021407-9
Rework -- Inspected 180 cases of SBX 750 product
120 cases of rework to be processed

People: 0 tardy
0 absent
70% perm. Hours
8.8 hours of setup time

Providing balanced performance feedback on a daily basis is perhaps the best way to develop an improvement oriented work culture that focuses on all areas of importance. My experience has taught me that the phrase "No feedback, no motivation" makes a lot of sense. If people only get feedback specific to their daily contributions on a weekly, monthly, quarterly, or annual basis, they will be relatively less motivated to improve. If feedback is only provided specific to a certain performance area, such as throughput, your people will be less likely to consider safety, quality, or morale measures to be as important as the measures that are mentioned more often.

I used the above daily dashboard to provide my people with performance feedback in the areas of safety, quality, people, and cost. Because I changed this information each day, and tried to present it in a manner that made it easy to read and understand, I found that my folks would actually look at it and comment about it. It also served as my key tool for tracking the daily waste events that affected the performance of the processes I owned. My maintenance people would even give me feedback about the accuracy of certain downtime events I would list!

Some people were interested in the details, but others were not. Almost everyone would look at the colors though – they knew that a 'four green' day was a great thing to accomplish. They also learned over time how different waste incidents, such as downtime, absences, or quality problems, affected the larger production system – the process itself. Even though most of them knew if they had experienced a good day or not when they left the plant each night, the daily dashboard helped explain WHY the day did not go as well as one might have hoped for.

A daily dashboard similar to this one can be created for any process. If the process does not have a daily cycle, you may not be able to give people cycle time feedback each day, but you can still let them know what the key waste events for the day were, what significant accomplishments occurred, and how the day's performance compares with past performances.

Most organizations are beginning to use the color code approach to reflect different levels of performance, and some are also looking at a variety of performance areas. A much smaller percentage however are actually giving people daily feedback in a manner that helps identify key waste areas, inspire higher levels of performance, and contribute to positive culture spin.

Great Systems!
"Simple systems, great results!"

NOTES:

Use It!

Improving Your Performance Analysis and Review Processes

- Build theories about factors affecting process trends

- Improve ability to spot the real problems needing resources

- Evaluate and identify how to know if your fixes really worked

Build theories about factors affecting process trends – Why are we getting better? Why are we not getting better fast enough? What process challenges are holding us back? Every day, thousands, if not millions, of explanations are offered about why a measure got better or worse than the day before.

In too many cases however, the explanations given are not based on data analysis – they are merely opinion. Even in those cases where data is used, it is not 'trend over time' based. This book chapter includes several exercises to help you improve your trend analysis skills.

Improve your ability to spot real problems – All too often, limited resources are invested in the wrong areas – areas where the cost of the investment is not justified by the benefit to be gained. This mainly occurs when we rely on only opinions, limited data sets, and/ or snapshot data to make our decisions. It is magnified when daily errors and defects are not tracked at the process level. How well do you know the magnitude of your process waste streams?

Using the right measures to measure the right things will help you make the right investment choices. Process-based measures are more sensitive to the impact of system changes. In turn, their use helps you spot and respond to indicators of problems – higher error rates, for example – before the bigger problems themselves, such as customer complaints, become a reality.

Evaluate the degree that fixes work – Corrective action impact is a common area where the wrong, or no, measures are used to gauge improvement effectiveness. Many will argue that the fixes worked as planned if the problem does not happen again, but which problems are they referring too – just the big problem, or also the 'smaller' errors that led to the 'perfect storm'?

Were all problems identified? How long will each fix remain effective? How do we know how well our processes are performing? How healthy are your processes? An effective performance analysis and review process asks questions such as these on a consistent basis.

Great Systems!
"Simple systems, great results!"

What Theories Can You Find?

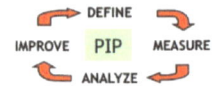

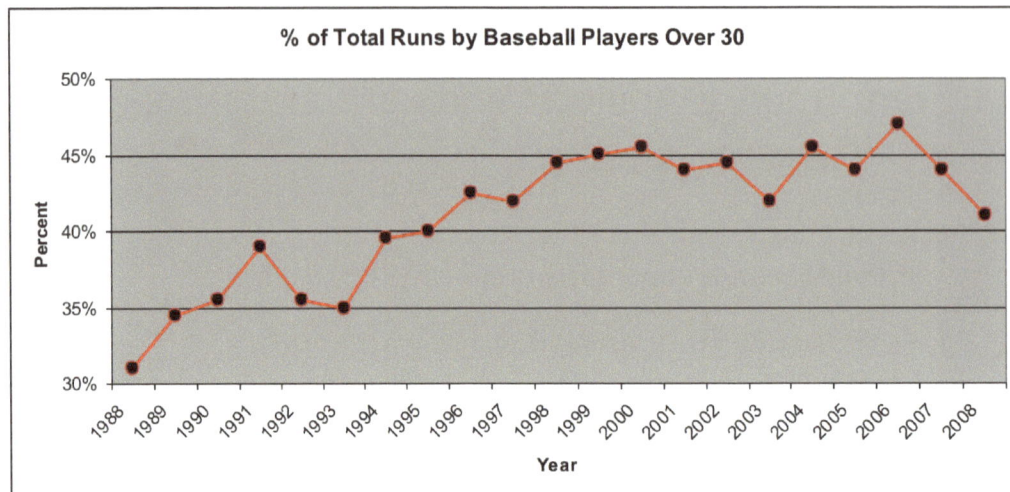

% of Total Runs by Baseball Players Over 30

Most organizations measure process output in their attempts to get more productivity from their assets. The world of sports is no different. In the above example, the percentage of runs produced by baseball players over the age of 30 was increasing, but now has leveled off, if not begun to decline. Our goal here is to develop theories as to why this is happening.

What are some possible theories to help explain this shift in performance?

- What are some systemic reasons that explain the ten-year increase (1988-1998) in the percentage of total runs produced by 'over 30' baseball players??
- What are some possible system factors that can cause the above ratio to level off, go up, or down over time for all ballplayers in general?
- What other types of data would you want to see to help better understand the above trend?

In this example, people are quick to assume that the trend line's behavior is primarily affected by the increase in performance enhancing drug use up until 1998, when the creation and enforcement of new rules began. There are however many other factors, such as new ballpark design, better nutrition and conditioning in general, and free agency rule changes, that also affected this trend line.

To better understand the behavior of this mixed measure, additional data would be needed. How has run production in general trended against this line? To what degree is the baseball workforce aging – what trend does the 'percentage of baseball players over 30' line reflect?

In addition to developing theories to understand past performance, it is just as key to create possible theories about expected future performance. What future behavior do we expect from this measure? What types of system changes can we make to influence that behavior?

How Might We Explain the Scoring Gain?

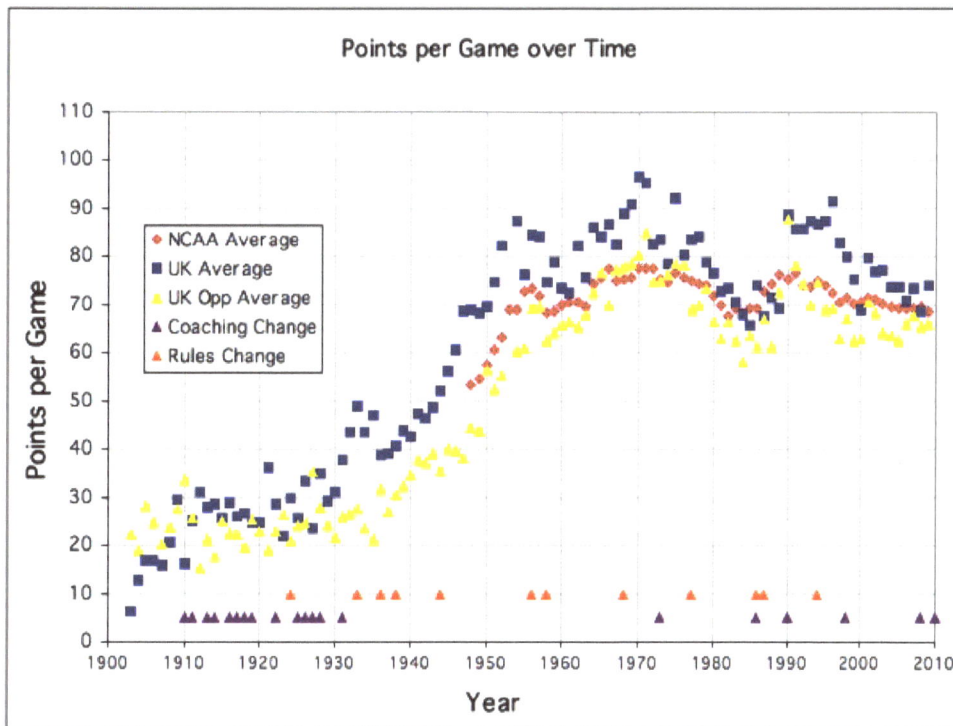

Points per Game over Time

In the previous example, the total time span involved was 20 years. In this example, we are looking at process output over 110 years of time. The above graph looks at points scored per basketball game for college teams overall versus the University of Kentucky and their opponents. The longer time horizon helps make the impact of system changes more evident.

Three trend lines exist for analysis in the above graph. Note that coaching changes and rule changes are also indicated in those years where they occurred at the bottom of the chart. Can you think of any college basketball rule changes that might have affected the average number of points scored per game? What might explain why Kentucky tends to consistently score more than their opponents, and the NCAA, on average?

What are some systemic reasons that explain the above trend? In other words, what factors do you think led to the points per game rate increasing for a period of time, and then decreasing and leveling off? Theories must be defined before they can be explored.

What are the different system factors that can cause the above ratio to go up or down? If you wanted to affect this ratio in order to increase fan satisfaction levels, what types of system changes would you consider? Which of these changes would have the greatest effect on point production?

What other types of data would you want to see to help better understand the above trend? How might you use a similar approach to examine your own process trends?

Key Process Analysis Steps

To analyze ANY process:

- **Define and measure to understand the process**

- **Use audits and trend lines to help find problems**

- **Use Pareto charts to help find and prioritize problems**

- **Use control charts to gauge process variation and trends**

- **Ask questions to help identify possible causes (use TapRooT® RCA if possible)**

> **DON'T mix data from different processes together!!**

All too often we take our processes for granted. We become comfortable, if not complacent, with the daily outcomes produced by our processes, whether those outcomes are desired or undesired. Problems that just won't go away are explained away instead – "That is just the way that process works" or "We've tried to fix that in the past, but there is no solution." Teams might be formed to drive process improvement, but we don't really expect to see consistent day-to-day improvement over time. We are trapped by our invalid stories from the past, but we believe these stories as if they are the truth, and the only truth.

Most of these erroneous ways of thinking and acting exist simply because we don't see the need to measure and understand work at the process level. We have somehow been fooled into thinking that we can measure at the department, plant, business unit, or company level and somehow affect meaningful process change. Unfortunately, I have rarely seen such a high level approach to process improvement work – we can get pockets of excellence, or spikes of improvement, but we struggle to sustain continuous improvement across all of our key work processes. What are we doing wrong?

My experiences have taught me that there is only one way to sustain continuous process improvement across all key processes – **require all process owners** to (1) capture their key daily counts and ratios and (2) capture and analyze key daily process problems. This approach has worked both for myself, and for others, who have used a similar approach.

Capturing daily process counts and ratios provides the data for developing trend lines and process behavior charts – essential tools for truly understanding a process. Capturing key daily process problems (errors AND defects), and using Pareto analysis to spot the truly big problems, provides direction for putting effective process changes in place.

Effective process-based measurement will not solve your problems for you, but it will help you choose where to use limited time and money resources more effectively. It will also give you a much better set of vital signs for telling the degree to which your fixes are working, or not working. Keep improving!

Predicting Future Process Outcomes

- **Most process outcomes will fall between +- 3 sigma 99.7% of the time**

- **All outcomes can be predicted, but the range of possible outcomes (the variation) is too great**

- **Reducing process variation is the key to accurate outcome prediction**

- **The '% sigma' ratio (1 sigma / mean) is a good indicator of process variability (lower is better)**

Reduce variation to improve prediction accuracy!

One day, I walked to the back of the assembly line at the start of the shift, only to see the team gathered around the daily production schedule. As I got closer, I noticed that they were tossing dollar bills onto the lead man's clipboard. When I asked them what was up, they said they were betting on what time code will be on the last bottle produced that day. When I asked them how close you needed to be to the actual time in order to win most days, their reply was quick – within five to ten minutes. The process had become that predictable.

By counting the number of batches, flavor changes, and size or container changes, and using one's knowledge of process capability, any team member could estimate when the schedule for the day was expected to be finished within five to ten minutes on most days. These folks did not know much about statistical process control, common cause versus special cause variation, or standard deviation calculations, but they had learned to trust the system through data analysis – if you know the inputs, you can project with reasonable accuracy what the outputs will be.

Most processes are typically in control. Per Shewhart's work, special cause variation only occurs 1% of the time, so we should not focus on eliminating these relatively rare occurrences as much as we should concentrate on trying to reduce process variation by putting process changes in place. Reducing variation (process width) makes a process more predictable.

The current variation from the mean may be significant – the % sigma is quite high in other words – but the process is still predictable. Unfortunately, most people are not comfortable with a prediction that could fall anywhere that is 50% above or below the mean. Instead, a % sigma of 1-5% is much better to work with from a prediction perspective.

To calculate your process's % sigma ratio, simply divide sigma (one standard deviation) by the mean. Again, processes with a high degree of variation are predictable, but the possible range of outcomes is too large to serve as a good predictor. Tighten up the variation however, and you should be able to estimate a range of future process performance values with 99% accuracy.

ICU Pharmacy Waste Incident Database - January 2006
Note: This database is used to track late deliveries (LD), order errors (OE), and NVA / lost work time (LT)

Date	Duration	Location	Waste Incident	What went wrong?	Cause Code	Waste Code
4-Jan	15	ICU Pharmacy	Tube system down / not working	Use alternative means to deliver	TD	LT
4-Jan	10	ICU 2	Late delivery of "list med type"	Tube did not send - hand deliver	TR	LD
4-Jan	22	ICU 6	Late delivery of "list med type"	Tube did not send - hand deliver	TR	LD
4-Jan	15	ICU 3	Late delivery of "list med type"	Tube did not send - hand deliver	TR	LD
4-Jan	35	ICU Pharmacy	Excess wait for order approval	Multiple pages to get approval	EW	LT
4-Jan	0	ICU Pharmacy	Order did not have two signatures	Pharmacy was short staffed	SS	OE
4-Jan	7	ICU6	Late delivery of "list med type"	Pharmacy was short staffed	SS	LD
4-Jan	17	ICU Pharmacy	Go out and collect tubes	Tubes were not returned to phamacy	NT	LT
5-Jan	19	NICU	Late delivery of "list med type"	Tube did not send - hand deliver	TR	LD
5-Jan	28	ICU 1	Late delivery of "list med type"	Tube did not send - hand deliver	TR	LD
5-Jan	19	ICU Pharmacy	Go out and collect tubes	Tubes were not returned to phamacy	NT	LT
5-Jan	21	ICU Pharmacy	Go out and collect tubes	Tubes were not returned to phamacy	NT	LT
6-Jan	23	ICU Pharmacy	Go out and collect tubes	Tubes were not returned to phamacy	NT	LT
6-Jan	30	ICU Pharmacy	Go out and collect tubes	Tubes were not returned to phamacy	NT	LT
6-Jan	31	ICU Pharmacy	Go get meds from Central Pharmacy	Meds not available in ICU Pharmacy	NM	LT
6-Jan	19	ICU Pharmacy	Go out and collect tubes	Tubes were not returned to phamacy	NT	LT
7-Jan	25	ICU Pharmacy	Tube system down / not working	Use alternative means to deliver	TD	LT
7-Jan	6	ICU 4	Late delivery of "list med type"	Tube did not send - hand deliver	TR	LD
7-Jan	11	ICU 7	Late delivery of "list med type"	Tube did not send - hand deliver	TR	LD
7-Jan	0	ICU Pharmacy	Wrong dosage of "med type"	Prescription was hard to read	UO	OE
7-Jan	0	ICU Pharmacy	Order did not have two signatures	Pharmacy was short staffed	SS	OE
7-Jan	16	ICU 5	Hand deliver to avoid late delivery	Tube did not send - hand deliver	TR	LT
7-Jan	28	NICU	Hand deliver to avoid late delivery	Tube did not send - hand deliver	TR	LT
8-Jan	15	ICU Pharmacy	Go out and collect tubes	Tubes were not returned to phamacy	NT	LT
8-Jan	20	ICU Pharmacy	Go out and collect tubes	Tubes were not returned to phamacy	NT	LT
8-Jan	27	ICU Pharmacy	Go get meds from Central Pharmacy	Meds not available in ICU Pharmacy	NM	LT
11-Jan	21	ICU Pharmacy	Go out and collect tubes	Tubes were not returned to phamacy	NT	LT
11-Jan	31	ICU 6	Hand deliver to avoid late delivery	Excess wait to approve order	EW	LT
12-Jan	22	ICU Pharmacy	Go out and collect tubes	Tubes were not returned to phamacy	NT	LT
12-Jan	31	ICU Pharmacy	Go get meds from Central Pharmacy	Meds not available in ICU Pharmacy	NM	LT
12-Jan	19	ICU Pharmacy	Go out and collect tubes	Tubes were not returned to phamacy	NT	LT
12-Jan	18	ICU 6	Hand deliver to avoid late delivery	Excess wait to approve order	EW	LT

As stated previously, *process-based improvement is the key to accelerated process excellence.* Process-based improvement is driven by requiring all process owners to (1) capture their key daily counts and ratios and (2) capture and analyze daily process problems (human errors, equipment failures, and defects). The error tracker database is the key tool to use for capturing key daily process problems.

Before computers, it was a lot more difficult to capture and analyze the key errors and defects for a given process on a regular basis. Now that we have spreadsheets and databases however that most people can learn how to use, we can easily capture and analyze those key problems that result in time or financial waste. I have used error tracking databases similar to the example shown above to reduce downtime, rework, product waste, freight claims, and customer complaints. Each process owner has to capture his or her problems daily for it to work however.

This tool is easy to use, but you have to be committed to capturing your key problems each day. Most organizations do a pretty good job of this when it comes to looking at recordable safety incidents for example, but it is rarely the case where each process owner can show you a similar database for the processes they are responsible for. What types of error tracking databases do you use in your organization? Are you using them to make improvements in all key performance areas, such as safety, quality, people, and cost?

Once you have set up the database, and made the commitment to capturing your key problems each day, you are in a position to use trending and Pareto analysis to identify high leverage waste areas. By using the sorting, query, and graphing functions that are common to software packages like Excel or access, you can easily produce charts that visually show you where your problem areas are. Don't discount the importance of creating the pictures. Look at the above example which is only sorted by date – can you easily spot where the problem areas are? What degree of loss is this process experiencing each day? No – we need pictures!

We often fail to recognize how significant a problem is until we analyze the frequency with which it is occurring and the duration of the occurrences. Instead, we grow complacent and begin to accept our process waste as just being the way things are. The error tracking database is the starting point for realizing where high leverage improvement opportunities exist.

Example Pareto Charts

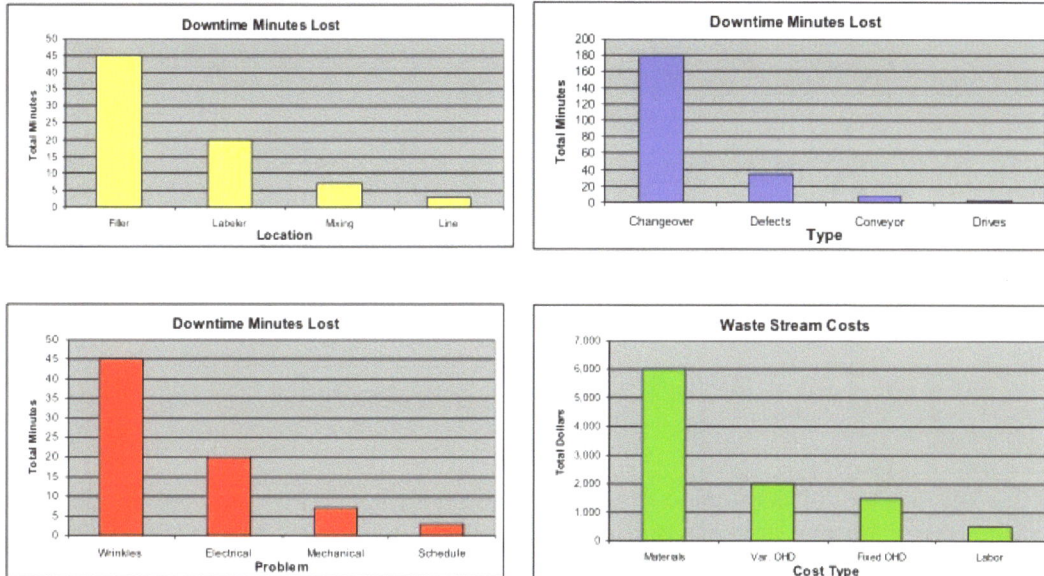

Pareto charts are one of the original seven basic quality tools, and yet today, many people do not know what a Pareto chart is. If you don't believe me, give it a try. Ask your leadership team members if they know what a Pareto chart is or not. Most of the process owners I have directed this question at do not know what a Pareto chart is by name, but when they see one, they do recognize the declining bar pattern – they have seen them before (just not very often).

In today's management performance review world, pie charts have taken the place of Pareto charts to a large extent. While both chart types reflect the same form of data analysis – they both give you a percentage breakdown by frequency or cost – I still favor, and recommend, Pareto charts over pie charts simply because **a difference in bar height is much easier to see than a difference in wedge width**.

Once you collected a fair amount of data (30 or more records) in your error tracking database, Pareto charts can be used to help you find high leverage improvement areas. Keep in mind that these charts can be of a % of cost or % of frequency nature. The norm is to create frequency-based Pareto charts, but any frequency Pareto can also be displayed in cost form if you know the cost of your errors! **Do you know what your key process errors cost you each day?**

Pareto charts are not trend lines – they only give you a snapshot of process performance. Their use is important however when it comes to determining which problem areas should have resources allocated towards their resolution. We would love to be able to fix all of our problems all at once, but that is simply not possible – we have resource limitations. Using Pareto charts on a regular basis will help you prioritize your process problems, in turn helping you make sure that the wheel that needs the grease gets it, instead of always greasing the one that squeaks the loudest. Do you know which process errors are causing you the most problems?

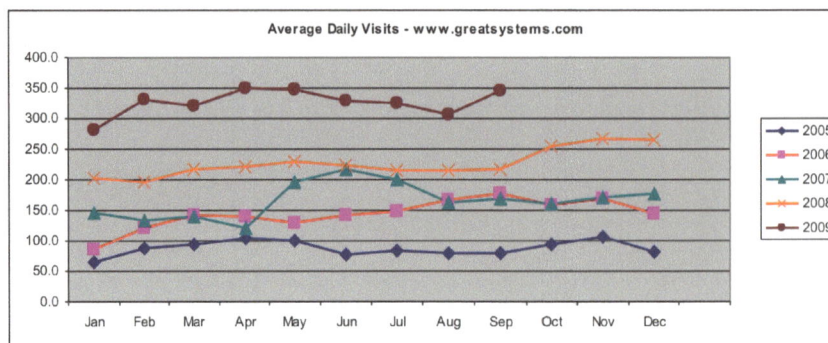

How effective are the systems you use daily?

One of the key challenges with using measures effectively lies in how you choose to display your data for reporting and analysis purposes. As with many quality tool applications, people tend to use charts incorrectly. They manipulate the vertical axis to make trends look better or worse. They lump multiple processes into one trend line, and then try to draw conclusions or build theories about what is affecting process performance. They change their control limits periodically, instead of waiting for the data to tell them when a limits change is warranted.

In a true continuous improvement environment, a given process measure should improve over time. For this reason, year over year (YOY) or month over month (MOM) charts similar to the one shown above are perhaps the best tool for gauging the degree that continuous improvement is actually occurring. In the above example, the goal is to consistently improve the number of website visits per day. While there are some months where this goal was not achieved, in general, the above process is exhibiting continuous improvement behavior.

Measure sensitivity, often defined by measurement frequency, plays a large role in properly assessing process performance over time. Measurement frequency SHOULD be determined by the process cycle time – the shorter a given process cycle is, the more frequently data can be obtained. Unfortunately, most measurement frequencies are driven by the time available to crunch the numbers or prepare the periodic report, or by simply what has been done in the past.

In the above example, 50 visits per day were occurring in the first year of measurement, and I like to try to get 20-30 samples per measurement period. A 'visits per hour' measure would be too sensitive, and a 'visits per month' ratio would not be sensitive enough. The nice thing is that if you are using a performance summary spreadsheet to capture key process counts, the time divisor in your formulas can be easily changed to make a given ratio more or less sensitive.

It is bad form to only have one line on a line chart – there is nothing to compare the actual performance level to in such cases. Performance goals, or best in class levels, can be used as a comparative line, but I have found making comparisons to past process performance to be more effective **as long as a goal of consistently improving process performance over time exists**. How do you use line charts to display performance trends?

Example Annotated Trend Line

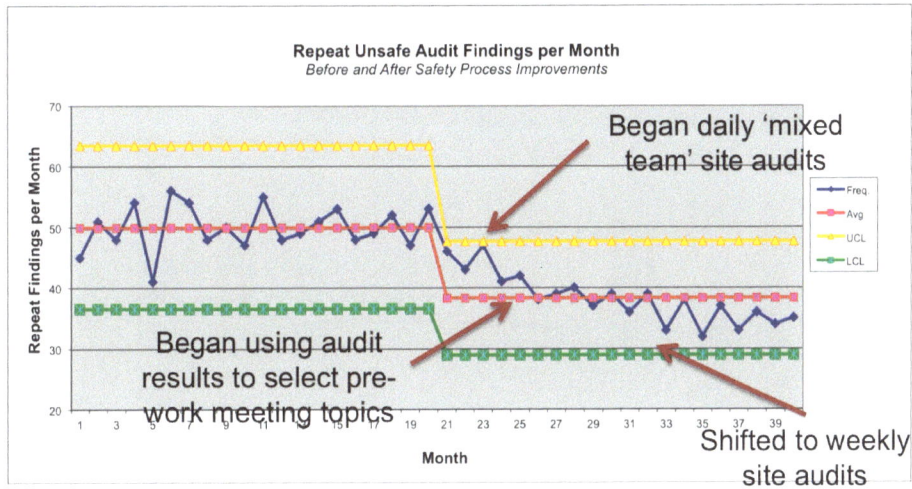

Repeat Unsafe Audit Findings per Month
Before and After Safety Process Improvements

Began daily 'mixed team' site audits

Began using audit results to select pre-work meeting topics

Shifted to weekly site audits

Shifts in process behavior should be visible!

If a process improvement or corrective action works, the impact of that change should theoretically be visible in the vital signs for that improved process. In reality, other process shifts – both known and unknown – affect trend line behavior as well. It is not uncommon for the benefits of a positive change in one part of the process to be wiped out by the loss of control to some degree in another part of the process. For example, increases in employee turnover can offset the benefits of improved safety training, resulting in no net change to the accident record.

To combat this challenge – to make the likelihood of being able to see the effects of your changes greater – you need to make sure that you are (1) measuring at the process level and (2) using a sensitive enough ratio. Ratio sensitivity is affected by type of count used (a leading error-based count is best), measurement frequency, and sample size. For example, well-designed near miss or behavior based safety programs provide much more sensitive potential injury data than simply tracking injuries alone.

In the above example, the count is of a 'leading error' nature, as repeat 'unsafe act' audit findings are being trended over time versus the injuries that such unsafe behaviors or conditions could cause. The monthly time frame being used is not the best, as the common month-to-month variation in days per month is often missed or misinterpreted. Something has caused the error rate to drop – it is difficult to assume from the above data however which specific process improvement, if any, was the most effective in reducing repeat findings over time.

Using a 'repeat findings per audit' ratio, and other scoring methods that apply increased point penalties for repeat findings, would be recommended as a start here. This is also why there is such benefit in tracking ALL key daily errors that occur at the process level for each process.

Improvement effectiveness should be visible in the trend lines for your vital signs. All too often however, we are not looking at the right vital signs, if process-based vital signs exist at all. How sensitive is your data? **How do you know if your improvements are really working?**

Can You Spot the System Changes?

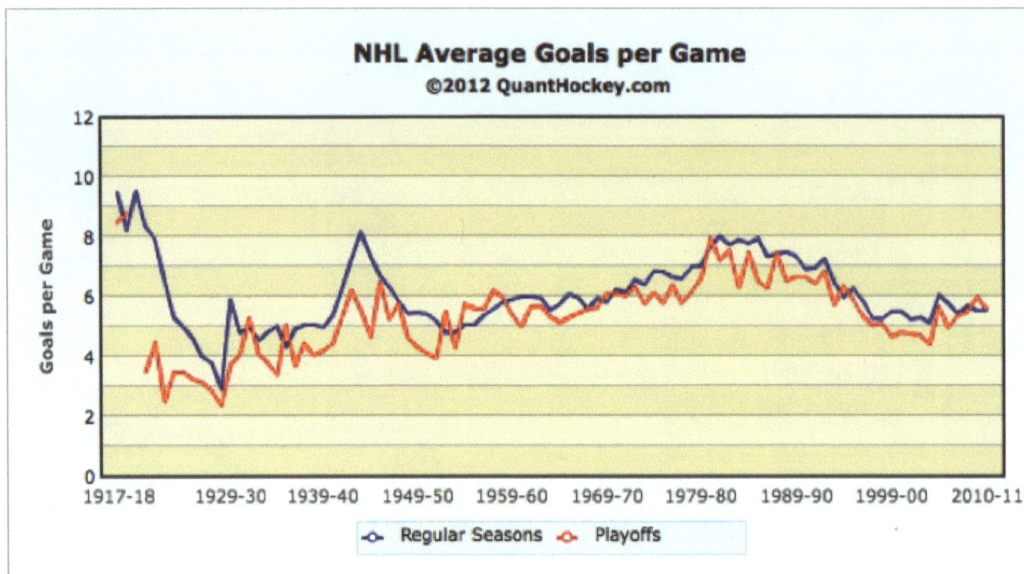

NHL Average Goals per Game
©2012 QuantHockey.com

Imagine that you were challenged with improving the above system. What are some of the first steps you would take? Hopefully, one of them would be to better understand the system, using trend analysis as a primary tool. If that is the case, try starting with the following questions whenever you are challenged with interpreting or improving the data shown on a chart.

What is being trended? In this example, we are looking at the game-by-game production from a collection of professional hockey teams (the National Hockey League). Both the title and the 'y' axis include the use of this ratio. The 'x' axis tells us that this is a time-based ratio that spans more than ninety years – a really long time in sports terms, and a very large sample size.

There are also two lines on the chart – output per game rates are shown for both playoff games and regular season games. Whenever you see two lines on a chart, you should be looking for additional relationship influences – when are the performances similar and when are they different? What gaps exist between the lines, and where are the gaps larger versus smaller?

How are the trend lines behaving? You may not have liked algebra in high school, but that is where you probably came across the equation for line slope – y=mx+b. Line slope tells us the rate of change occurring in a system for a given point in time. Steeper sloped lines imply that the rate of change is relatively greater. Looking for gaps between the lines should also be performed, as line gaps offer the opportunity for theory building and best practice identification.

How significant is the degree of change shown? In the above chart, the general increase in scoring over time, both during the regular season and the playoffs, is what stands out the most. In fact, over the time period shown, team output increased from less than three goals per game to eight goals a game – 167% - between league inception and the 1980s!

The drop in team performance following that 1980s peak is also worth exploring – what rule changes and other system shifts might explain the drop in output that occurred in the 1990s?

How Many System Changes Do You See?

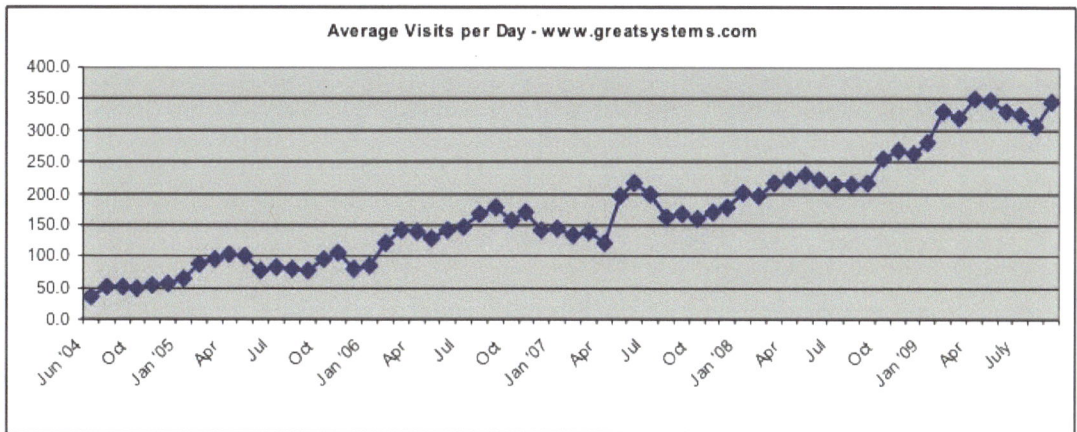

Average Visits per Day - www.greatsystems.com

What control limits would you use?

Traditional control chart use was associated with maintaining tight dimensional, temperature, or pressure tolerances during a given production process. As long as the actual process results stayed within the defined limits, the process was considered to be in control. Today, it is more common to be pursuing a goal of maximizing, optimizing, or minimizing at zero, a given process measure. Staying the same is not an option, or goal, near as much as it used to be.

Because the type of process application is different, control charts need to be used differently for them to be effective in helping to minimize process variation and better predict future performance results for most process types. For example, a moving range chart will typically meet most process measurement needs from a control charting perspective.

In the above example, systems change is occurring so rapidly that the trend line does not flatten out. Such process behavior is common in rapidly growing sales territories and business that are expanding in volume quickly. Can control limits be drawn when a system appears to out of control all of the time? They can, but you need to chart the change in the growth itself.

One solution would be to base your control limits on the rate of change from month to month, instead of on the number of visits per month. This means that the slope of your control limits would parallel the slope of the process average. Such a chart would help predict future growth rates with the existing systems or to identify when new changes have begun to affect performance results.

Process trend lines help you monitor your key process vital signs more effectively because performance shifts, gaps, relationships, and rates of change are more visual. Adding control limits to any trend line help you better understand the current range of performance outcomes that are possible and identify when improvement efforts really are making a difference. Without control limits, it is very difficult to understand and process performance. You also can't tell if you are reducing process variation and making the process more predictable.

Great Systems!
"Simple systems, great results!"

Learning by Separating Systems

September Website Visits

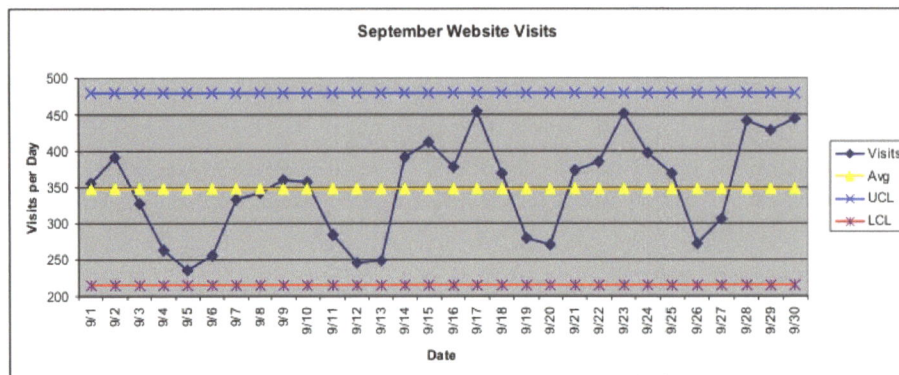

Probably the biggest measurement system mistake that organizations make is to combine multiple processes into one process behavior curve. When this done, unrelated variation is typically introduced into the picture. In the above example, two different processes (at least) are represented by the single trend line – weekday website traffic and weekend website traffic. This combination of multiple processes is creating the peaks and valleys of behavior and encouraging the erroneous definition of problems that are not really problems.

Measures are often grouped because the occurrence frequency of the lagging indicator in use is too low for the uncombined charts to stand on their own. For example, this often happens with personal injury or employee satisfaction data in smaller organizations or work groups.

When this does occur, you should not combine processes into one chart as a solution. Instead, start using a more SENSITIVE measure to gauge process performance in a given performance area. For example, switching from a lagging indicator like patient complaints or equipment failures to a more proactive patient satisfaction score, preventive maintenance task effectiveness score, or error rate might help you avoid needing to combine reactive indicators.

We also combine systems to avoid having to create too many charts. This belief is leftover from the 'before computers' days when colored pencils, graph paper, a ruler, and an eraser were needed to draw charts. Today, with the use of Excel pivot tables and other analytic software, we can quickly create a variety of graphical looks for a myriad of process measures. In fact, your challenge really should be deciding which measures BEST reflect true process performance in all areas of importance, and how those counts or ratios can be captured in a lean manner.

Always start at the process level and work outwards. This is the only way to better understand how the behavior of a given process can affect the larger work system, or systems. Some processes cancel out the performance of other processes. In other cases, one process can magnify, if not accelerate, the performance of others. Such relationships are quite difficult to detect if (1) your measures are not sensitive enough to shifts in process performance and (2) you are combining the performance of multiple processes into one measure.

Attempting to explain (build theories) around process behavior using system-level trend data is a waste of time. With today's technology, there is no excuse for not improving your data mining skills. What charts do you need to break apart in order to better understand a process problem?

86

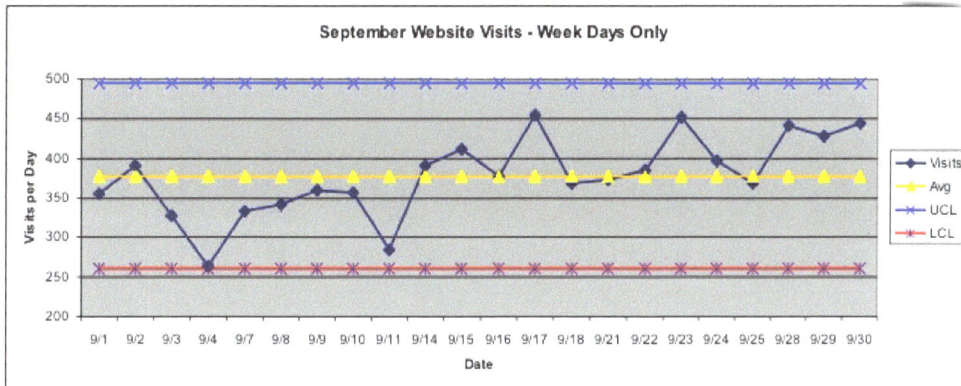

September Website Visits - Week Days Only

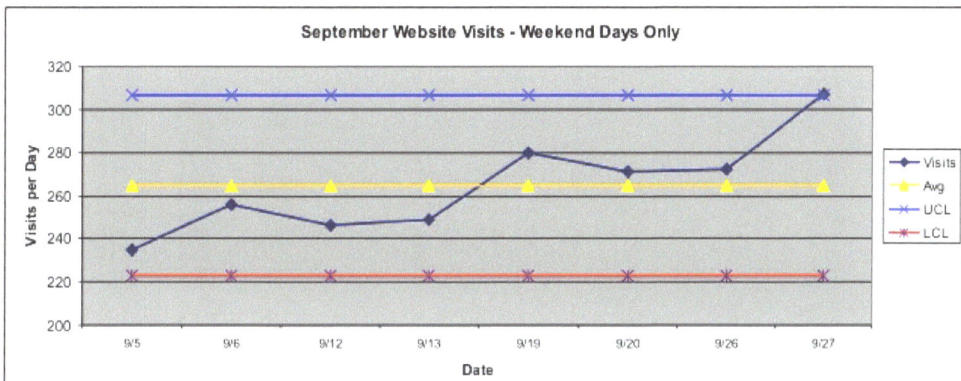

September Website Visits - Weekend Days Only

In the above two charts, we have separated the two systems that were graphed together on the previous page. Now that two distinct charts have been created, you can see that the process behaviors are very different. The growth trends are similar, - the systems are related - but the growth pattern is more erratic, and the visit rate is higher, with weekday website traffic. This makes sense for a business website.

Pivot tables are a quick way to organize and analyze tables of data, and possible scenarios based on that data, in Excel. As with any data analysis tool however, you must first collect the right mix of counts at the process level (and otherwise) to fuel this analysis. For example, in many cases, it is difficult to measure process cost because costs are only captured at the cost center level – they are not allocated back to the processes that actually incur these costs. Process owners often have to set up their own estimated costing system to help get cost ratio data for the processes they own.

The slope of a line and its percent sigma value are two key indicators that system or process mixing is occurring on a chart. If a line is overly steep (high slope) or flat (variation washout), it is worthwhile to explore what is causing such line behavior – is it the data being used or is it systems change? Similarly, a percent sigma value over 25% indicates high variation, and even variation percentages of greater than 10% deserve attention. Percent sigma, by the way, is derived by dividing the standard deviation of a given process measure by the process average.

Teams need to practice building theories about their own performance results, just as they need to continue to improve their data capture and crunch processes. Enhanced systems understanding will lead to improved decision making and more effective corrective actions over time. What performance review and analysis improvement needs have you identified?

Great Systems!
"Simple systems, great results!"

NOTES:

Improve It!

Recognizing Performance Improvement Success

- Use effective formal approaches to recognize process-based improvement

- Help focus daily efforts on the right types of tasks and enhance decision speed / quality

- Enhance process measurement – improvement - compensation linkages

A lot of data is captured, only to go to waste, in too many organizations. In other words, too much data is not used, or is used incorrectly, on a daily basis. How do you, or others, use the data you are responsible for collecting each day? For example, if you do audits that are designed to identify non-conformances and assess the degree that a process is in compliance, what becomes of the audit data you capture and turn in on a given audit form? How often do you see data being used to enforce the wrong, versus the right, on the job behaviors?

Use formal approaches to effectively recognize process-based improvement – Numbers give us something to talk about each day, good or bad. Numbers also give us ways to recognize good performance both informally – with a meaningful thank you – and formally – via some sort of giveaway. While the best recognition will always be some form of daily, positive, consistent, and meaningful thank you, *number-based formal recognition processes can heighten a team's interest in daily performance, and their focus on performance improvement*, as well.

Focus daily efforts on making the right choices, and enhance decision speed and quality – The squeaky wheel all too often gets the grease. We react, and in some cases over react, to the wrong numbers, trends that are not really there, and worst of all, opinion, all too often. Many managers make multi-million dollar decisions daily without looking at the right vital signs first. How well do you use your numbers to support formal decision-making efforts? How well do you understand process behaviors - do you know where your process bottlenecks are?

Improve your process measurement - improvement - compensation linkages – What gets measured gets done. No feedback, no motivation. These sayings explain a lot when it comes to understanding how numbers can affect human behavior. The problem is that we use the wrong numbers, we measure the wrong things, and we use the numbers we do capture incorrectly. The way we currently use our numbers is driving behaviors the wrong way in many cases! Look at the design of your profit sharing plan – what types of measures are in the plan, what are the probabilities of attaining the different goals that were set (and how were they set), and what types of personal actions are required to qualify for a given level of compensation?

Great Systems!
"Simple systems, great results!"

Example Profit Sharing Worksheet

% of Profit Contributed =	10%

Performance Area			Jan	Feb	Mar	Apr	May	Jun	Jul
SAFETY **25%**	**OSHA Reportable Accidents**								
	Actual for Month		1	0	2	0	0	1	0
	Goal		0	0	0	0	0	0	0
	% of Goal Achieved		75%	100%	50%	100%	100%	75%	100%
	Profit Share Earned		$18,750	$23,750	$13,875	$12,500	$21,875	$4,688	$19,450
QUALITY **25%**	**Rework Pounds %**								
	Actual for Month		10.3%	9.9%	11.0%	10.5%	10.7%	9.8%	9.9%
	Goal		10.0%	10.0%	9.9%	9.9%	9.8%	9.8%	9.8%
	% of Goal Achieved		75%	100%	0%	50%	25%	100%	75%
	Profit Share Earned		$18,750	$23,750	$0	$6,250	$5,469	$6,250	$14,588
COST **25%**	**Cost of Goods Solds per Pound**								
	Actual for Month		0.880	0.873	0.869	0.910	0.850	0.899	0.902
	Goal		0.870	0.870	0.870	0.865	0.865	0.865	0.865
	% Over / Under Goal		1.1%	0.3%	-0.1%	5.2%	-1.7%	3.9%	4.3%
	% of Goal Achieved		75%	75%	100%	0%	100%	0%	0%
	Profit Share Earned		$18,750	$17,813	$27,750	$0	$21,875	$0	$0
PEOPLE **25%**	**Total Absenteeism**								
	Actual for Month		2	5	1	6	0	4	1
	Goal		0	0	0	0	0	0	0
	% of Goal Achieved		75%	25%	75%	0%	100%	50%	75%
	Profit Share Earned		$18,750	$5,938	$20,813	$0	$21,875	$3,125	$14,588
	Performance Adjustment Factor		75%	75%	56%	38%	81%	56%	63%

Is your measurement system driving the right behaviors? What gets measured gets done, especially when a percentage of our pay is determined by the performance of those things being measured. It is a good thing to give every deserving employee a percentage of the profit when an organization succeeds, but even more ownership is gained as the link between daily work and such pay is strengthened. As an example, explore the design of the above profit sharing plan spreadsheet. What types of performance are important in this organization?

Performance Area Selection and Weighting - In the above profit sharing spreadsheet, you can see that an equal weight of 25% has been placed on the four key performance areas of Safety, Quality, Cost, and People. Determining these weighting assignments is one of the more difficult, but insightful, activities that make up the measurement system design process. What we emphasize, and attach emotion to, reflect what we consider to be important. Reaching consensus on key performance areas, vital signs, and pay links can be an emotional event.

Key Measures for Each Performance Area – Notice that one key performance measure has been defined for each key performance area. You can attach more than one measure to a key performance area if you wish to indicate additional importance, but we kept it to one measure per area in this example for simplicity.

Payout per Measure – There is a potential maximum amount of payout for each measure that can occur using the above plan design. The owners decide what percentage of profit will be placed in the profit pool. The number of employees on the plan is the second factor that affects payout, and the number of performance areas, and area weighting, are the third and fourth factors to consider. The number of measures is the final determining factor.

The above design is simple, but it is a great place to start. Keep in mind that line of sight – the time between profit share payouts – also matters. Quarterly or monthly payouts work best.

Setting Up a Color Assignment-Based Recognition Approach

Recognize records or goals realized – Several examples exist for linking scorecard use to team recognition. The first example, which is color assignment based, is presented below. We have already seen an example of an advanced scorecard, where points are assigned based on the level of performance that is realized (page 52). This second approach requires more time to set up, but it does provide a more quantitative and progressive approach for linking team performance to levels of recognition. The use of color has become common in organizations.

The celebrations and forms of recognition should become more significant as the point total rises or the 'percent of green colors possible' attained increases. For example, if the maximum number of points possible on a scorecard is 300 points and you are currently at 200 points, you might want to set 25 point milestones. Whenever you score between 225 and 249 points, you might want to bring in doughnuts or fruit. A performance score between 250 and 274 points might warrant a pizza party. Breaking the 275 point barrier might result in everyone getting a "We broke the barrier" T-shirts.

With the more basic color assignment approach shown below, the type of recognition provided to the team varies with the percentage of green colors gained during a given period of time. For example, if the team achieves green levels of performance 75% of the time, they might receive $50 worth of doughnuts or fruit. Achieving an 85% green performance level might result in a $150 pizza party for the month. If the team achieves a 95% green performance level for the month, they might receive t-shirts that commemorate the accomplishment, or you may want to simply give a $10 gift certificate to each team member.

'Go for the Green' Recognition Plan

GREEN	YELLOW	RED
No recordable or first aid accidents	First Aid accident	OSHA recordable accident
No absences or tardies	One absence or tardy	More than 1 absences or tardy
No product placed on hold	One hold occurrence	More than 1 hold occurrence
Under the budgeted cost per case	Up to 5% > the budgeted cost per case	5% or more over the budgeted cost per case

Each month, the following formal recognition options exist (4 points / day possible):

95% of possible points	$300 – Cookout or T-shirts
90% of possible points	$200 – Pizza, chicken dinner, or subs
85% of possible points	$100 – doughnuts, fruit, or sodas

Creating and using scorecards should be a team effort. The process will not work if people do not take ownership in it. Involve as many people as you can in selecting key measures, assigning weights, and even in deciding what strategy you should use to set the performance ranges. Most importantly, use their ideas to make improvements!

Great Systems!
"Simple systems, great results!"

Vital Signs, Scorecards, and Goals

The first step in setting up a color assignment scorecard-based recognition process is to define the different levels of performance that will lead to a green (good), yellow (average), or red (poor) color assignment for each of the performance areas. You may recall that we talked about ways to do this earlier in the book. In the previous example, notice how the performance expectations differ across key performance areas as the possible point levels change.

Once the color assignments have been determined, you are ready to begin to evaluate performance each day against these levels, using a tool such as the daily dashboard that was presented earlier. The key here is to give your team daily performance feedback, so that they know how they are doing and have a visible goal to shoot for as the month progresses.

In the following example, the team achieved 100% of the green assignments that were possible for the Safety performance area during the month. 79% of the People green assignments, 53% of the green Quality assignments, and 32% of the green Cost assignments were also captured during the month, for a total 'green' percentage of 66%. In this example, the team would not earn any recognition for the month based on overall performance, but the supervisor may still want to recognize the superior safety results that were obtained.

Example Monthly Recognition Scores

"Go for the Gold"
Recognition
Program Results
for April 2013

	Safety	People	Quality	Cost	Pts.
4/1	0	1A	0	0.65	14
4/2	0	2A	237	70 / 1.54	8
4/3	0	1A	227	0.7	10
4/4	0	0	158	0.6	14
4/8	0	0	0	0.75	14
4/9	0	0	282	0.78	12
4/10	0	0	24	1.03	12
4/11	0	0	0	9 / 9 / 7	14
4/12	0	0	0	0.74	14
4/15	0	0	0	0.58	14
4/16	0	0	668	1.7 / 1.0 / .58	12
4/17	0	0	0	0.72	14
4/18	0	0	0	0.63	20
4/22	0	0	0	0.58	20
4/23	0	1A	0	.67 / .76	14
4/24	0	0	69	81 / 1.48	12
4/25	0	0	0	0.59	20
4/29	0	0	1,272	1.1 / 71	12
4/30		0	125	0.69	12

The objective of this process (game) is to score more points each month. This will not happen by simply asking people to work harder or be more careful. Instead, they will need to be actively involved in making process improvements. They might also participate in formal problem solving teams to help identify improvements, evaluate options, and put the best option in place.

Over time, you will establish performance records. You will also need to define when it is time to change the performance ranges you have set (i.e. quarterly or annually). Fine tune the process so that it works for you, and don't be afraid to make your own enhancements.

High performance organizations normally link scorecard use directly into the profit sharing compensation system that exists in the organization. The most effective version of such an approach involves making some form of monthly payout to employees at all levels based on the performance results for that month. The level of payout varies with the degree of success that was realized in each key performance area. Area weighting is used to determine what percentage of the profit sharing pool is associated with each performance area.

The '100 Point' Club' Approach

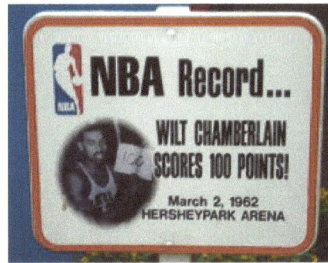

Earning Monthly Points

Perfect Attendance = 5 points

Accident Free = 15 points

KPI Goal Achieved = 25 points

Earning Extra Points

Idea Submitted = 5 points

Project Team Work = 100 points

Losing Points

Recordable Injury = – 100 points

Unplanned absence = -10 points

Spending Points

Logo Hat = 100 points

Logo Jacket = 250 points

Flat Screen TV = 1,000 points

Gift Certificates = $.50 / point

Tool Box and Tools = 500 points

The '100 Point Club' formal recognition approach is a great way to recognize all employees who achieve certain levels of performance. Its structure helps avoid favoritism as formal recognition is given, and employees are given the flexibility of selecting from a range of gifts as well. Points can be redeemed at any time, depending on the value of gift desired.

In the above example, most employees earn some amount of points monthly. Extra points can also be earned for submitting improvement ideas or participating on a process improvement team. Points can be lost for recordable injuries and unplanned absences. Because the process is simple, different recognition scenarios can be simulated using historical data to help structure the plan so it focuses the right amount of points on the right types of performance.

Here are some key questions to ask when designing a formal recognition system:

- What percentage of the workforce do I want to formally recognize each year? What percentage of the workforce do I want to recognize more frequently than once a year?
- What is my total formal recognition budget? If I recognized all employees, what would the annual recognition amount per employee equal?
- What performance goals are the most important? Which goals do I have the greatest probability of realizing based on the improvements that are planned?
- What types of activities should earn a person extra points? How do I make sure that all employees have an equal opportunity to earn these points?
- What types of performance should people lose points for? How often should we expect this to happen?
- What types of formal recognition approaches have we tried in the past? What worked and what did not? How can we do things differently this time to avoid the challenges we experienced in the past?

The 'Helmet Sticker' Option

In football, helmet stickers are earned for:

- Scoring and wins
- Achieving specific team goals
- Reaching workgroup goals
- Academic achievement

If you want to use stickers for recognition:

- Define how stickers can be earned
- Make earned stickers visible
- Hand out stickers weekly or monthly
- Consider using special stickers

Helmet stickers work similarly to points in that you earn them for doing good things. Gifts are not part of the recognition program however in most cases – it is privilege enough to earn the stickers. Don't think that your people need to wear hard hats or helmets at work in order to use this approach however – earned stickers can be placed on a wall mounted tracking board or locker just as easily as they can be placed on a helmet or hard hat.

Stickers are given out in football for realizing individual or team goals. For example, everyone on the team might get a sticker for a win, but only the offensive personnel get stickers for surpassing the one hundred yard rushing milestone. One person might get a sticker for recovering a fumble. Different colors and icons can be used to signify a different focus – academic stickers are given out by some college teams to complement the more game oriented 'sticker winning' criteria. The Georgia Bulldogs, for example, give out white dog bones and black dog bones to recognize exemplary performance both on, and off, the field.

Because the cost per person for the sticker recognition approach is lower than other recognition approaches that include regular giveaways, stickers can be given out more often. You don't want to dilute their meaning, but *it is more effective when you can recognize great work contributions on a weekly or daily basis versus only monthly, quarterly, or annually.*

Many other ways exist to recognize employees. The first step most people take is to replace any 'one winner' focused approaches with 'qualified winner' approaches. This means criteria for receiving a given type of sticker, award, or gift need to be defined. Most programs need to be expanded to include all employees – formal recognition is still much too limited in many organizations (such as only sales gets formal performance awards).

Use the new data you are going to capture, and your new data analysis tools, to find the best program for your company. Spreadsheets offer a great way to simulate the financial impact of different recognition program configurations, helping you to reach more people with a more meaningful, positive, and consistent 'thank you.'

94

Final Thoughts on Using Measures to Recognize Performance

The following three steps are key to making a numbers-based recognition process work. Formally recognizing performance will have little value if each employee does not understand (1) how his or her work affects the company numbers and (2) what actions can be taken personally on a daily basis to help improve team and organizational performance.

Set up a visual daily dashboard and monthly scorecard – Having a daily dashboard and scorecard in each work area makes team vital sign performance visible. An example daily dashboard was shown and explained on page 73. To make the monthly scorecard visible to all, you can simply recreate a larger version of the scorecard form provided later in this workbook, or you can set up a smaller version that does not include the performance ranges. In either case, weights, measure names, and actual performance results should be displayed. Be sure to show the most recent score, the current record, and "point total" trends on your scoreboard.

Scoring is easy, and necessary, to link formal recognition to the approach. Once you have received actual performance results, identify how many points that level of performance earned. To add emphasis to a performance area, consider multiplying the number of points earned by the measure's weight to get your score for that measure. Remember that what gets measured and promoted gets done – what is formally recognized fits into the promotion category!

Define the formal recognition process -- Be sure to create operational definitions and process flow charts for each recognition system process. These "rules of the game" are mandatory for fairness, understanding, and problem solving. Identify key data inputs, calculation methods, what is needed to achieve different levels of recognition, and recognition / award options.

Begin the process -- Kick off your recognition process by explaining to everyone how the process works, why it is necessary, and how they will be involved in it. Use recent performance examples to help illustrate the tradeoffs between measures and why balance is needed. Most importantly, identify "point total milestones" that will create the need for celebration!

On the next two pages, you will find two additional examples of tools that can be used to help complete the balanced scorecard and goal setting aspects of the "Use It" phase.

> ## Win the Race Each Day!

- ◎ Did I capture key errors and pass ZERO defects on to my customer?
- ◎ Did I avoid injury to myself and others?
- ◎ Did I support my team when they needed me?
- ◎ Did I work in a consistent, effective manner?

What is your team's winning percentage?

Scorecard Setup Worksheet

By completing this worksheet, you can make the initial decisions necessary for scorecard setup. This worksheet can be used to set up a company, workgroup, or personal scorecard. If you are using control limits to set your performance ranges, consider giving the UCL a value of "8" and the LCL a value of "2."

Performance Range Data

Key Performance Area	Wt.	Key Measure	Avg.	Max	Min	Int.

Example Year-to-Date Scorecard

Process Team : _____

Process Owner: _____

Month	Reportable Accidents	Absences and Tardies	Calls per Labor Hour	% Problem Calls	% Dropped Calls	% in 5 seconds	Cost per Call	Total Points Earned
Jan	0 - 5 pts	0 - 5 pts	20.5 - 5 pts	13% - 5 pts	0.7% - 5 pts	91% - 3 pts	.60 - 3 pts	31 / 35 pts
Feb	0 - 5 pts	2 - 3 pts	19.2 - 3 pts	16% - 2 pts	1.0% - 3 pts	90% - 3 pts	.65 - 0 pts	19 / 35 pts
Mar	0 - 5 pts	5 - 0 pts	18.9 - 2 pts	15% - 3 pts	1.1% - 2 pts	88% - 2 pts	.58 - 4 pts	18 / 35 pts
Apr	1 - 2 pts	4 - 1 pts	21.0 - 5 pts	12% - 5 pts	0.8% - 5 pts	93% - 4 pts	.62 - 1 pts	23 / 35 pts
May	0 - 5 pts	6 - 0 pts	20.2 - 5 pts	14% - 4 pts	0.8% - 5 pts	86% - 1 pt	.56 - 5 pts	25 / 35 pts
Jun	2 - 0 pts	1 - 4 pts	19.4 - 3 pts	17% - 1 pt	1.0% - 3 pts	92% - 4 pts	.59 - 4 pts	19 / 35 pts
Jul								
Aug								
Sep								
Oct								
Nov								
Dec								
YTD	3 - 22 pts	18 - 13 pts	19.9 - 23 pts	15% - 20 pts	0.9% - 23 pts	90% - 17 pts	.60 - 17 pts	135 pts - 64%

Customer Requirements and Measures

* >90% answered in 5 seconds
* < 1% dropped calls
* > 20 calls per labor hour
*> 85% information calls
* Own the call
* Seek first to understand

Great Systems!
"Simple systems, great results!"

NOTES:

Improve It!

Performing Measurement System Check-Ups

- Improve measure selection, performance review, and goal setting processes annually
- Evaluate benchmark validity for gauging plan execution
- Enhance process measurement - formal recognition linkages

As with the ten different physiological systems that exist within each of our bodies, the health of our work systems must assessed on a regular basis. In the world of work, the bulk of such assessment should occur as part of the annual planning process. Effective triggers should also be in place however to alert managers to possible process-level performance challenges before they grow too large. Measurement system checkups are critical to keeping that system healthy.

Improve measure selection and goal setting processes annually – The performance, design, and effectiveness of certain work systems should be reviewed at least annually by the Senior Leadership team. Three key numbers-focused work systems that fall into this review category are the measure selection process, the performance review process, and the goal setting process. Such reviews are typically performed as part of the annual planning process, before actually being used to select measures, review performance, and set goals for the coming year.

Evaluate benchmark validity for gauging plan execution effectiveness – Benchmarks can be used to define short and long term performance goals. They represent our vision of what a perfect day looks like – how our processes would perform if we had a day with no problems and lots of great performances. Many organizations don't currently use external benchmarks, and often the internal benchmark comparisons that are used involve comparing systems that are actually dissimilar. Use your organization's mission and vision to define the type of benchmarks needed, and then begin identifying them and putting them to use as a performance review tool.

Enhance process improvement – formal recognition linkages – Too many formal recognition programs recognize only a small percentage of people for doing things that are often part of the daily job. If many organizations are using the wrong measures, recognizing people for the wrong things, or recognizing the wrong people, limited or ineffective recognition is a natural outcome. Similarly, bonus systems that emphasize one area of performance over others will alter daily work behaviors in a not necessarily good way. We get what we pay for, whether we recognize what we are really paying for or not. What types of performance are your leaders really rewarding each day?

Great Systems!
"Simple systems, great results!"

> **Annual Measurement System Review Areas**

◉ Right Key Performance Areas (KPAs)?

◉ Right Mix of Counts and Ratios?

◉ Measure Selection Process

◉ Performance Review Process

◉ Goal Setting Process

◉ Recognition Process

**User feedback is key to improving
process performance!**

Right Key Performance Areas (KPAs)? – Performance areas typically do not change that much from year to year, as they usually reflect the organization's mission, vision, values, core competencies (those things you are really great at), and strategic intent. The performance areas in use should still be reviewed annually, just as the mission, vision, values, core competencies, and strategic objectives should be, as part of the annual planning process.

Right mix of counts and ratios? - Most companies have too many lagging counts in their performance measure mix. Ideally, leading ratios should make up the bulk of your key measures. As all counts can usually be converted into ratios, counts should be used only on a limited basis as a vital sign or as part of your key measure mix. Use ratios instead.

Measure Selection Process Effectiveness? – How structured is your measure selection process? Have you drawn a flow diagram of it? How does the use of this process help ensure that vital signs have been defined for all key processes? How do you know that use of the selected measures is driving the right behaviors and types of process improvement?

Performance Review Process Effectiveness? – How do you use your numbers on a regular basis – typically monthly – to identify performance gaps and strengths? What is done with the information that comes out of these reviews? How could the design of your performance review meetings be improved to help make them even more effective?

Goal Setting Process Effectiveness? – Are you like most organizations when it comes to goal setting – do you simply take last year's average, bump it up by a percentage, and say 'Go for it'? Performance goals should be based on performance expectations, process capability, and the types of changes that are planned to improve process performance. *All goals have a probability of being realized – system design is what truly affects this probability of success.*

Recognition Process Effectiveness? – Are your measures driving performance improvement in the right areas? Are you effectively recognizing **all** of your strong performers, and are your measures helping to identify human performance gaps where improved system design is needed? Can your people consistently define what a great or 'perfect' day at work looks like? Can they describe the vital signs that they look at daily to find 'evidence of greatness'?

100

Improving Your Measurement System

Here are eleven key ways to create a high performance measurement system:

- Identify key performance areas, such as safety, quality, cost, and people
- Use work groups to identify key performance metrics for each performance area
- Identify sources and definitions for each key metric (process feedback)
- Use a spreadsheet to collect and chart key data over time
- Construct line and control charts for each key metric
- Post and update performance charts regularly in all work areas
- Teach others about how to use the charts and what they mean
- Use work groups to identify and prioritize theories for improving performance
- Monitor improvement results on your line / control charts
- Continue to drive out special cause variation and reduce common cause variation
- Work to lower the system average once variation has been reduced

Your primary goal should be to make sure that the right types of process-based measures are selected and used for all key work processes. Selecting the right measures will help you achieve your second goal, which is to gain consistent application and understanding of the basic measurement system, and the processes to be improved, by all workgroups. You may also want to improve your measurement systems further by streamlining your data collection efforts, defining even more meaningful measures, and identifying / clarifying additional performance tradeoffs. Lean data capture, effective data crunching, and meaningful data use should be your goal.

You will also want to increase the linkage between your company planning efforts and your workgroup process improvement activities. Doing this will help your project teams and management groups better define how to spend limited project resources on those improvement areas that would benefit from their application the most. By keeping this process simple, focused, and visible, this goal can be obtained.

The need may also exist to establish a total cost picture. After the initial phase of your improved measuring efforts, you will have a much clearer understanding of how you spend your labor and other expense dollars. Additional work is needed however to define a clearer 'total cost' of process errors and servicing your customers. As cost vital signs are identified, the related spreadsheets and scorecards should be modified to include a total cost component for each work team. Activity-based costing is one effective approach to help you achieve this goal.

Additional learning and practice may also be needed by management to learn to use Excel spreadsheets or other data capture and analysis software. Initially, one person might be primarily responsible for modifying most of the workgroup spreadsheets and graphs. To make the process really effective, these skills need to be learned and used by all members of management. Over time, they can also be transferred down to the front lines.

Great Systems!
"Simple systems, great results!"

Possible Deployment Action Items

- ☒ Decide which formal leaders will track process-based measures
- ☒ Determine how measurement system effectiveness will be reviewed annually
- ☒ Use measures to predict process performance
- ☒ Create plan to shift towards activity based costing
- ☒ Provide business literacy training
- ☒ Share best practices to help achieve lean data capture

Keep the process simple, focused, and flexible

Decide which formal leaders will track process-based measures – Making this choice might sound simple, but **the choice you make will be fundamental in determining how fast these tools begin to affect change in your organization**. Ideally, you will see all work as process, and in turn, expect all process owners – all formal leaders – to capture key process data daily, crunch that data at least monthly, and lead their people in making true system changes that improve process performance, for the processes they own, over time.

Determine how measurement system effectiveness will be reviewed annually – The best organizations review key work system performance at least once a year. This is usually done as part of the annual planning process – improvement days are often held once a year for this purpose as well. The key is that you take a look at the types of measures being used, what you are measuring, and how you are using those measures to improve performance.

Use measures to predict performance – As data quality improves and error reduction helps reduce the variation in your key process measures, you will be able to more effectively predict future process performance. This is possible at any time, but the range of possible outcomes due to excessive variation makes prediction somewhat irrelevant. Variation is the smoke, not the fire. If your variation is too great however, there is a process error fire burning somewhere.

Create a plan to shift towards activity-based costing – Improved process data will also help you better determine what your true cost drivers are. Once your process cost drivers have been identified, they can then be optimized to better meet customer requirements.

Provide business literacy training – People understand, and try to reduce, waste levels to a greater degree when they are expressed in financial terms. Linking daily work efforts to daily process costs helps provide incentive to reduce process waste streams.

Share best practices to help achieve lean data capture – Measurement systems evolve over time, so don't expect to be able to select the right mix of measures, measure just the right things, or use measures exactly right the first time. Formally sharing best practice efforts however helps spread change more rapidly as people build on the ideas of others.

102

Possible Deployment Challenges

➜ Low computer literacy in places

➜ Low business literacy in places

➜ History of using measures as "a hammer"

➜ Multiple location and positions

➜ More complex than just "one number"

➜ "I don't have time" – meeting and e-mail waste

➜ "This too shall pass"

Typically, job descriptions, personal performance measures, and compensation goals must be changed

I have helped people install, or at least attempt to install, measurement systems at over fifty different locations, so I have heard most of the reasons why this type of change can't be done. The most common failure points exist where middle and/or upper management does not support the change to the degree that they should and where daily process measurement is not built into each process owner's job. The biggest excuse these days – "I don't have time."

People are going to resist change. This natural resistance is only heightened when past changes 'like this' have resulted in job loss, excess overtime for little value, multiple 'slogan of the month' contests, or simply more stress. Natural resistance to doing things that involve numbers and math also exists with many people, which only heightens the stress and resistance. Patience and persistence is needed to get over these cultural hurdles, with sincere educational efforts being made to bring everyone up to speed.

"I don't have time to collect more numbers or analyze problems" is a common excuse people use when asked to measure more at the process level. As they are currently spending their time, such statements are true. It might also be true that a significant percentage of those current time expenditures are not as value added as they could be. *Typically, by reducing e-mail and meeting waste with a significant system change or two, it is easy to find time for measurement, analysis, and improvement in any job.* It depends on how one defines value.

When I am asked what it takes to change a culture quickly, I offer three key places to start. First, job descriptions must be changed to reflect the new and modified competencies that are needed as a result of the system changes being made. If possible, show time requirements as a percent of total time of job to reflect relative task importance in these modified job descriptions.

Second, identify measures (ideally ratios) that can be used to gauge job performance in each key area. For example, 'Capture key process counts and problems on a daily basis' and 'Analyze and summarize process performance on a monthly basis' are examples of performance objectives I have seen used before. Third, change the pay – performance link.

Great Systems!
"Simple systems, great results!"

The Formal Recognition Spectrum

Giveaways to Individuals	Performance Based Points Program	Team-based Performance Plan	Multi-level, integrated Recognition System
Individuals are given awards for performing certain tasks or making key contributions	Individual recognition is driven by team and personal contributions in a variety of areas	Monthly recognition based on team performance for a balanced set of performance results	Variety of individual and team-based recognition types awarded on both a regular and special case basis

- Individual or team?
- What to recognize?
- Whom to recognize?
- Award frequency?
- Award mix?
- Award value?

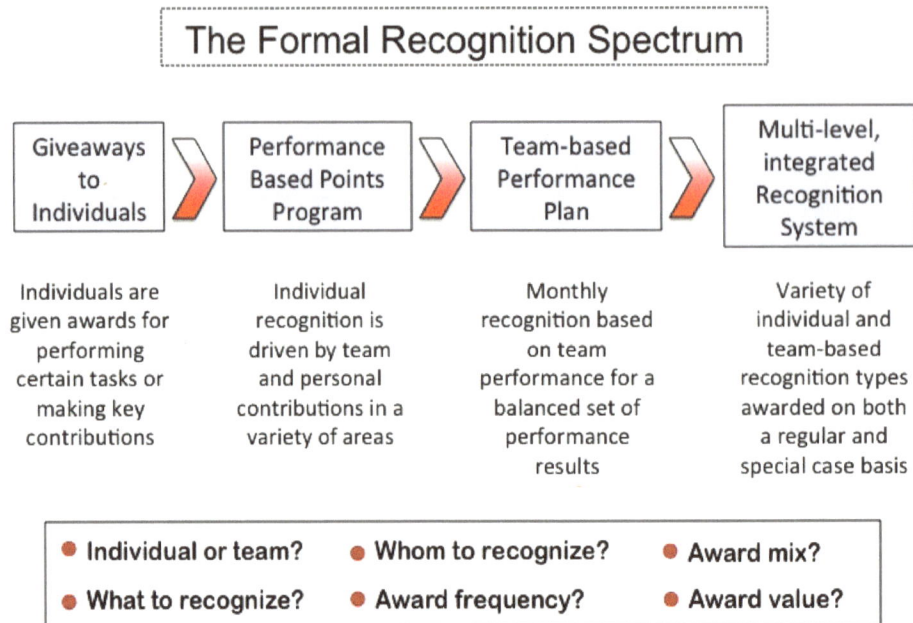

If you attempt to change everything all at one time, there is little chance that you will be successful. Small organizations can make big changes in months, but it sometimes take years to overhaul a measurement system in large organizations (if such an overhaul is even possible). Technology, however, will help accelerate this change.

Expect 3-5 big changes a year to be made, with all process owners making a similar contribution. Define the changes that are coming in the future, and even tell people about the upcoming journey, but don't force too much change to happen at one time. It is much more effective to engage more people and expect them to change at a reasonable rate than it is to expect a few pilot groups to install the whole system over a weekend.

Also plan for consistent and significant improvements in how people use informal recognition on a daily basis. This form of recognition is more meaningful when done correctly, and in turn, more powerful. I have seen organizations teach all employees Covey's 'Seven Habits of Highly Effective People' for the purpose of achieving this goal – learn to deliver meaningful, positive recognition on a daily basis. Bob Nelson's '1,001 Ways to Recognize Employees' is another great resource for formal recognition options.

The first thing many companies need to do when it comes to recognition is stop using 'one winner' recognition systems such as "Employee of the Month". They made successful comedies with such a focus, so something must be wrong with singling out one person when a team effort is needed for success. *The solution is to recognize anyone who meets the standards for recognition that have been defined.* We rarely see 'Perfect Attendance' recognized via a one winner recognition process design – no, we recognize everyone who achieves the goal.

The lack of fairness in the way a recognition process is designed or used is perhaps more damaging then failing to recognize enough people when a goal is achieved. Excellent recognition systems do not have to be complicated as much as they have to be fair, linked to the goals of the organization, and aligned with the daily tasks each person does to contribute.

104

Strive for Perfect Days, Every Day

⊙ What vital sign levels need to be achieved for perfection?

⊙ You can expect perfection, but it is rarely sustainable

⊙ Instead, expect your perfect day % to improve over time

⊙ Perfect day levels or ranges exist for any type of vital signs

What percentage of your shifts or work days are 'perfect days'?

One way to gauge your progress towards creating a proactive work culture is to track the number of perfect days a given person, team, or site has. When I bring up this metric in groups, which by the way is in use at a few 'big oil' companies as a key measure, the first question people ask is naturally "What is a perfect day?" Well, ask yourself that question – "What does a perfect work day look like when it is over?"

A perfect day can be what you want it to be, but generally, a perfect day occurs when no major defects (of any type) interrupt product or service flow – a day with no problems. Ideally, you have defined vital signs already for the process or person you want to measure, and these vital signs are in alignment with the person or process's goals. Vital sign levels define perfect days.

At my syrup plant, a perfect day occurred when we had no product placed on hold (Quality), no one was absent or tardy (People), no one was injured (Safety), and efficiency rates were met and no unplanned downtime was experienced (Cost). What would a perfect day look like in your world of work? How many process failures or errors a day do you allow to happen?

Since our plant worked 250 days a year on average (we rarely worked on weekends and we did get holidays), we saw this set of 250 days as a season. In a given planning year, we had the chance to win 250 games – a win could be a perfect day or simply doing well on a day that was pretty tough to achieve by the current standards. Each day, our vital sign performances would determine if we won the day, tied the day, or lost the day, as performance ranges had been pre-defined for each level of outcome.

The monthly winning percentage became a closely watched number. Perfect days were celebrated on the rare occasions they occurred, and as time went on, we had a few more on average than we used to have. Of course, zero perfect days is not that hard to beat … or is it?

What is your team's winning percentage? What scores do your vital signs need to be at in order to have a perfect day? What performance ranges for each vital sign would define a daily 'win?'

Great Systems!
"Simple systems, great results!"

Deploying Open Book Management

NOW

Get the Information Out There	Teach Business Literacy	Empower others and build ownership	Provide a Stake in Success and Failure
Post information in current form regularly and explain what it means	Teach others when the opportunity arises	Involve others when possible to help make improvements	Add profit shares into the current labor agreement
Link cost information to month-to-month scorecard performance	Provide training to manager and supervisors, who might train others	Use performance reviews in work group settings to identify key projects	Align profit sharing for all managers and supervisors
Provide additional financial performance information on a real-time basis	Provide actual business literacy training sessions	Form project teams around high leverage improvements needs	Place all employees on the same profit sharing plan
Create a 'huddle system to share and discuss information	Build business literacy into a broader training curriculum	Extend 'huddle system to include all employees, along with project teams	Offer stock ownership to provide a long term goal and focus

FUTURE

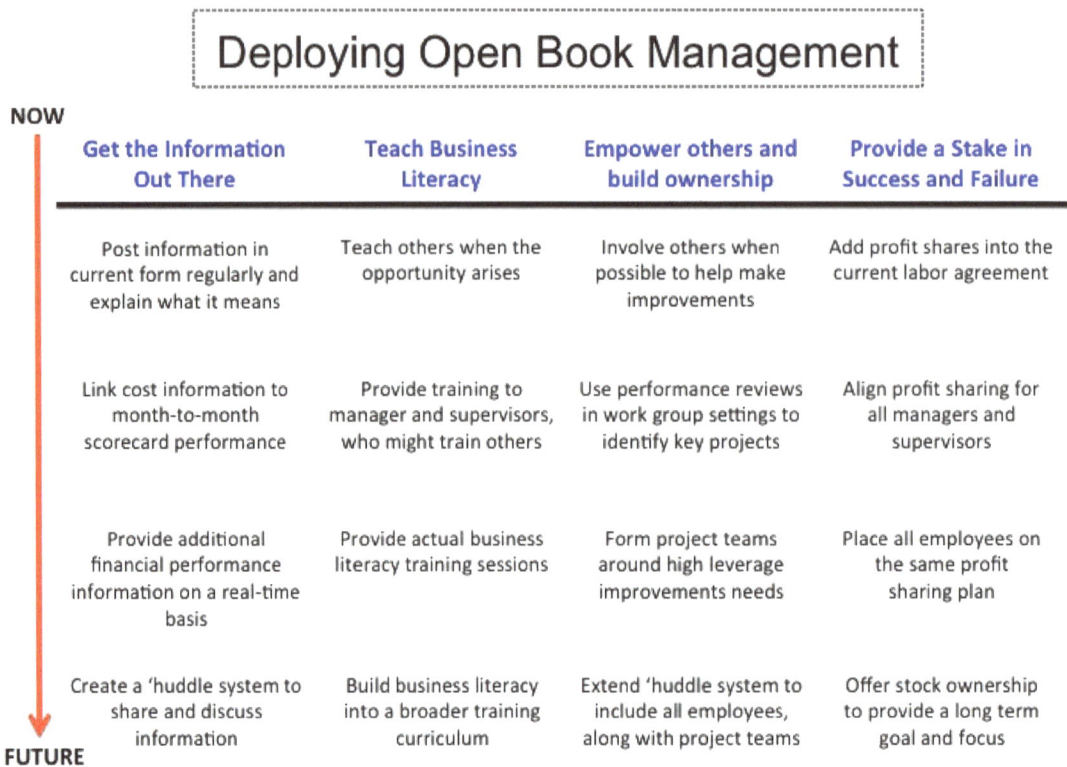

Whether you know it or not, by getting every person to at least look at process-based vital signs each day, you have begun the journey towards fully deployed open book management. Open book management is a concept that originated in the early 1990s when Jack Stack used it to help turn around the Springfield Remanufacturing facility in Missouri. "Get the information out there' is one of the key OBM first steps to take, as shown in the diagram above.

Performance reviews, pre-job huddles, and improvement teams are three areas where numbers should be used daily, or with each process cycle, to identify performance patterns and relationships. These techniques can also be used to help empower others and build ownership relative to improving daily process performance. As time progresses, you may even want to teach your people about how the organization makes and loses money – a business literacy extension that goes beyond simply understanding the daily process costs that exist.

Most importantly, you should strive to continue to build on the initial "open book management" concepts that you have put in place. Your biggest hurdle to doing this will likely involve extending the profit share program to all employees, or putting one in place if it does not already exist. Creating an Employee Stock Ownership Plan (ESOP) was also recommended by Stack to help create a longer-term stake in the organization's success or failure. If you organization is unionized, such changes will be even more challenging, but they still can be accomplished.

The open book management process works because it is simple, because each employee is involved with its setup and use, and because action is taken to deal with the "tough" issues that exist regarding performance measurement and improvement. Should you choose to give this process a try, feel free to modify and enhance it to meet your needs. Also recognize however that belief and behavior change, especially on the part of upper management, is requisite for its lasting success and bottom line impact.

Activity Based Costing Example

Cost Center / Function	Cost / Year	Cost Driver	Product A Factor	Product B Factor	Product A Multiplier	Product B Multiplier	Product A Cost / Unit	Product B Cost / Unit
Purchasing	$60,000	Units Produced	20,000,000	16,000,000	56%	44%	$0.003	$0.004
Raw Material	7,000,000	Pounds / Unit	2.50	1.50	68%	32%	0.236	0.142
Supplies	200,000	Units Produced	20,000,000	16,000,000	56%	44%	0.010	0.013
Utilities	260,000	# of Production Days	150	200	43%	57%	0.006	0.009
Direct Labor	300,000	Units Produced	20,000,000	16,000,000	56%	44%	0.015	0.019
Maintenance Parts	545,000	Total Line Hours	1,500	3,000	33%	67%	0.009	0.023
Maintenance Labor	250,000	Total Line Hours	1,500	3,000	33%	67%	0.004	0.010
Sales and Marketing	3,000,000	Units Produced	20,000,000	16,000,000	56%	44%	0.150	0.188
Human Resources	150,000	Standard Headcount	20	10	67%	33%	0.005	0.003
Info Technology	200,000	# of Production Days	150	200	43%	57%	0.004	0.007
						Total Cost per Unit =	$0.443	$0.417

What is really driving the costs that are spent daily in your different cost centers?

I really think that our cultural aversion to math is keeping activity based costing from taking root in more organizations. To me, it is a common sense way to help understand where your expenses are really being spent and what the real profit margins are for key product and service lines. To many it seems that activity based costing takes too much effort, is too complicated, and requires too much time. If you are capturing the right process counts each day however, it is pretty easy to at least estimate what your key cost drivers are – just do a little regression analysis (create a few scatter diagrams) and test a few theories.

Ideally, cost breakdowns by process type should readily available. We know how to do this with direct labor, and we are getting much better at allocating (assigning) our indirect labor to those processes that required such services. We still struggle however when it comes to assigning our fixed and many variable overhead costs to processes in the value stream. For example, how do you assign the cost of your engineering staff to a given product or service line that they support?

Activity based costing is not meant to be an exact science however. It is more important to (1) identify the key cost drivers for each cost center and (2) improve the processes that affect each cost driver. Completing a table similar to the one above can help you better understand where your expense dollars are actually going and what factors really influence cost performance over time. Often simply having your exempt staff track time percentages by project or product type can teach you a lot, once a few weekly trends have been established.

You may find that certain services are carrying too much overhead burden, and in turn, their profit margin is understated. Conversely, it is also likely that certain processes are not carrying their fair share of key expenses, and in turn, are being seen as profitable when they actually might be dragging down the overall profit margin of the organization. Activity-based costing, just like home budget analysis, can be very enlightening.

Great Systems!
"Simple systems, great results!"

Installing a Measurement System

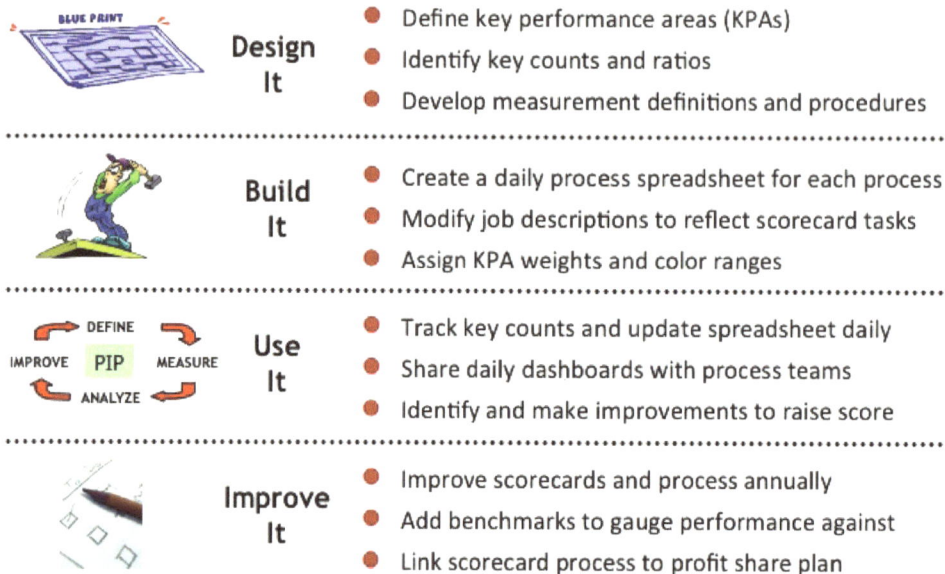

Design It
- Define key performance areas (KPAs)
- Identify key counts and ratios
- Develop measurement definitions and procedures

Build It
- Create a daily process spreadsheet for each process
- Modify job descriptions to reflect scorecard tasks
- Assign KPA weights and color ranges

Use It
- Track key counts and update spreadsheet daily
- Share daily dashboards with process teams
- Identify and make improvements to raise score

Improve It
- Improve scorecards and process annually
- Add benchmarks to gauge performance against
- Link scorecard process to profit share plan

On this page and the facing page, you will find multiple action items that are part of installing a high performance measurement system. The above visual takes the steps in the same order as they were presented in this book. The visual on the facing page looks at changing an organization's measurement system as well, but at a slower rate.

It may seem like a big step to make this type of change all at once across a business unit or even a site, but are the costs of the less than optimum decisions you might be making absent of meaningful measures? If nothing else, consider doing the "What's Your Measure Mix?" exercise, and notice how many of your current key performance indicators are lagging counts. Wouldn't a better mix of leading ratios serve as better indicators of current strategy success?

Are you really looking at the true vital signs of your key work processes? How often are you making expensive decisions with an incomplete, or wrong, data set? Could you be leaving profits on the table simply because certain errors and waste types go unrecognized, if not accepted as normal? If you answered 'Yes' to any of these questions, you might want to consider looking at some better indicators of process performance.

There are five key benefits to gain from improving your measurement system:

Increased service focus – One key reason I began using balanced scorecards was to help expand and shift the performance focus in the organizations where I worked. Previously, these locations had a tendency to focus mainly on efficiency figures (versus service or quality), as this data was the easiest to obtain and had the closest tangible connection to the bottom line (dollars). How well do your leaders balance the need for service with the need for efficiency?

By creating a reporting tool that (1) allowed regular performances in five or six key performance areas to viewed at the same time and (2) provided a total performance score, members of management were conditioned over time to look at the bigger picture.

Cycles of Improvement	Improving Your Measurement System

At Start	● Define key performance areas for your company
	● Identify key processes to be measured
	● Identify waste incidents types for all processes
First Cycle	● Create balanced scorecards for all key processes
	● Set up performance summary spreadsheets
Second Cycle	● Set up waste incident databases
	● All process owners track process performance
Third Cycle	● Define process capability for all key processes
	● Link measurement findings to the planning process

Improved trend recognition – Using the performance summary spreadsheet forces process owners to look more closely at their day-to-day performance numbers, and in particular, the relationship between work performed, hours worked, errors and effects generated, and dollars spent. Instead of relying solely on computer-generated reports that really do not show trends very well, many of these leaders can gain a better understanding of their performance trends simply by entering daily performance data into the spreadsheet and reflecting on their entries as they are made. Getting closer to the data helps enhance process understanding.

Higher systems understanding – This benefit will be visible with both the front line employees and management. The front line employee will be able to better see how his or her daily job impacts each performance area, primarily because he or she can see how the data they collect each day is used. Management benefits by gaining a clearer picture of the tradeoffs that exist between the various performance areas. This perspective helps identify optimum points of operation and improves overall value stream performance predictability.

Bottom line performance improvement – Work groups that understand and use process-based measurement will demonstrate a significant improvement in their scorecard measures. These gains can be attributed to increased performance measure visibility, a tighter linkage between daily actions and process results, the need for system improvements that effective measurement helps identify, and enhanced recognition of personal efforts and challenges.

Increased ownership – Momentum will build over time if this process is used correctly. Because people can explain how their daily job impacts the bottom line, and because they feel like management better understands their job, ownership will increase. In those groups where this process has been implemented to the greatest extent, each team member can explain what they have done to realize performance gains, and they can describe future actions that are planned to improve performance even more. They can also share the "headaches" that have been eliminated by the improvements they have suggested and helped put in place.

Great Systems!
"Simple systems, great results!"

How the Best Improve Their Measures

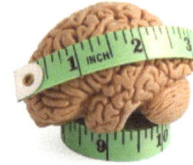

- Key process counts are captured daily
- Daily dashboards and trends are visible to all
- Measures are tracked and trended in several key areas
- Improvements and changes are linked to trend lines
- Key errors, defects, and causes are captured daily
- Mechanisms exist to alert people of process 'failure'
- Fact-based root cause analysis helps identify improvements
- Process performance is reviewed at work team meetings
- Data capture and crunch methods are reviewed and improved

As an Alumni Examiner for the Malcolm Baldrige National Performance Excellence Award, I have been able to witness the use of some simple, but great, measurement systems. Also, over the past thirty plus years, I have been directly involved with process measurement, process analysis, and process improvement approaches that worked to a large extent, but also had their learning moments. Fifty locations later, I know that meaningful measurement is possible.

I admittedly made more mistakes than I would have liked to have made as I experimented with different measurement system designs over the years – you don't need to make those same mistakes. There are effective design practices that help keep you from learning the wrong way.

I have tried to include all of the common attributes of great measurement systems I have seen in the above list. I have tried to include examples of these approaches and others that can help make measurement systems actually work. It really all boils down to these three things:

Right measures – Are you using leading ratios as your primary type of measure? Are you using percentages, time, and currency to essentially convert ANY count into a meaningful ratio? Are you capturing key counts daily, turning them into ratios, and trending them over time?

Right Place - Are you capturing key counts daily for each key process? Have you broken your existing 'mixed systems' charts apart so that the process behaviors they reflect are more meaningful? Are you switching to more sensitive measures, such as daily process non-conformance or human error rates, to help better understand individual performance?

Right Use – Are you beginning to use measurement to predict future performance instead of using numbers to look backwards into the past? Are you changing the way numbers are used to reward, reprimand, and otherwise influence behavior in the workplace?

Systems give you what they are designed to give you, and this is definitely true for measurement systems. Simple, well-designed measurement systems are needed however if sustained high performance through continued process improvement is a goal. Keep improving!

Scorecard Process Checklist

Listed below are the most common actions required to set up the scorecard process. Use this checklist to gauge your progress should you choose to implement this approach in your company or workgroup.

Measurement Setup   *Have you ...*

☐ Defined five to six key performance areas?

☐ Identified one or two key measures for each performance area?

☐ Created operational definitions for each performance measure?

☐ Defined data inputs, collection frequencies, and calculation methods?

☐ Used historical data and SPC to define process capability / boundaries?

Scorecard Setup   *Have you ...*

☐ Assigned weights for each performance area?

☐ Established performance ranges for each key measure?

☐ Aligned each performance range with annual goal expectations?

☐ Used historical data to test the scorecard's possible results?

☐ Ensured that scorecard setups are linked between workgroups?

☐ Achieved the desired level of balance between performance areas?

Process Roll-Out   *Have you ...*

☐ Put in place daily data collection systems, such as personal performance journals?

☐ Used computers wherever possible to avoid manual data collection & crunching?

☐ Set up a means of visually displaying daily and YTD performance trends?

☐ Provided basic training on how the process works?

☐ Linked recognition systems to the scorecard process?

☐ Built scorecard review into regular workgroup meeting agendas?

☐ Established a process for reviewing scorecard results and making adjustments?

☐ Integrated the process into each employee's daily job?

Great Systems!
"Simple systems, great results!"

Scorecard Implementation Action Plan

Action to Take	Start Date	End Date	By Who?

Defining Personal Next Steps
Total Time: 30 minutes

Objective: Define the next steps you should take when you return home to begin using the concepts and tools you have learned about during today's workshop.

Key Questions:

1. As a result of the work we have done today, what actions do I need to take?
2. Of these actions, which ones need to be addressed first?
3. Given the other job responsibilities I have, when can I expect these changes to be made – what would my measurement system improvement action plan look like?

Individual Tasks:

1 minute	1.	Review the material we have covered today
9 minutes	2.	Identify at least three next steps you should take to begin using what you have learned today

Report Out: 20 minutes for the large group report out   *20 total minutes*

As part of the report out, individuals in the workshop will be asked to volunteer 1-2 examples of next steps that they have personally identified. As the next steps are shared, you might want to capture those that you might use yourself.

Key Next Steps I Will Take to Begin Putting Great Measurement Systems in Place:

1. _____

2. _____

3. _____

4. _____

5. _____

6. _____

7. _____

Great Systems!
"Simple systems, great results!"

References and Recommendations

Abernathy, William "Balanced Scorecards Make Teamwork a Reality." *The Journal for Quality and Participation*, Nov / Dec 1997.

Cunningham, Keith J., "Keys to the Vault", Enclave Publishing, 2006. www.keystothevault.com

Deming, W. Edwards, "Out of the Crisis", W. Edwards Deming Institute, 1982.

Deming, W. Edwards, "Profound Knowledge", SPC Press, 1992.

Kaplan, Robert S. and David P. Norton "The Balanced Scorecard - Measures That Drive Performance." *Harvard Business Review*, Jan-Feb 1992.

Kaplan, Robert S. and David P. Norton. "Putting the Balanced Scorecard to Work." *Harvard Business Review*, Sep-Oct 1993.

Kaplan, Robert S. and David P. Norton. "Using the Balanced Scorecard as a Strategic Management System." *Harvard Business Review*, Jan-Feb 1996.

Kohn, Alfie "Punished by Rewards: the Trouble with Gold Stars, Incentive Plans, A's, Praise, and Other Bribes" Houghton Mifflin, 1993.

Paradies, Mark and Unger, Linda "TapRooT®: The System for Root Cause Analysis, Problem Investigation, and Proactive Improvement, System Improvements Inc., 2000

Schuster, John et al. "The Power of Open Book Management: Releasing the True Potential of People's Minds, Hearts, and Hands" John Wiley and Sons, Inc., 1996.

Stack, Jack "The Great Game of Business - Unlocking the Power and Profitability of Open-Book Management", Crown Publishing Group, 1992.

Wheeler, Donald "Understanding Variation: the Key to Managing Chaos", SPC Press, 1993.

Wheeler, Donald "Making Sense of Data", SPC Press, 2003.

Willyerd, Karie A. "Balancing Your Evaluation Act." *Training*, March 1997.

Bigbluehistory.net - The Kentucky Basketball Statistics Project

ESPN the Magazine and ESPN.com

Fivethirtyeight.com – leading edge analytics / analysis of sports, science, economics, and politics issues

Grantland.com – Sports and pop culture form a rotating cast of writers

Personal Performance Journal

Process :_____   Process Owner: _____

Date	Hours Worked					
1						
2						
3						
4						
5						
8						
9						
10						
11						
12						
15						
16						
17						
18						
19						
22						
23						
24						
25						
26						
29						
30						
31						
Totals						
Month: _____	Customer Requirements and Measures					

Great Systems!
"Simple systems, great results!"

Year-to-Date Scorecard

Process Owner: _____

Process Team : _____

Month	Reportable Accidents	Absences and Tardies						
Jan								
Feb								
Mar								
Apr								
May								
Jun								
Jul								
Aug								
Sep								
Oct								
Nov								
Dec								
YTD								

Customer Requirements and Measures

Summary Scorecard Worksheet

Company or Facility : _____

Operating Year: _____

Key Performance Areas

Team	SAFETY	QUALITY	COST	PEOPLE		

Great Systems!
"Simple systems, great results!"

117

Example Value Creation Processes, Requirements, and Measures

Value Creation Process Area	Key Customer Requirements	Key Processes and Tools	Key Process Measure(s)
New Product Development	Improve product features Develop new products Reduce production costs	Development process Customer listening posts Performance review process	Development cycle time Development cycle cost New product success %
Sales and Marketing	Retain current customers Attract new customers Maintain account accuracy	Account development process Customer targeting process Account updating	Customer retention % Revenue growth % Customer satisfaction index
Customer Service	Prompt response to calls Accurate information Timely information	Order entry process Information retrieval process Complaint resolution process	Call abandonment rate External survey score % calls answered in 10 sec.
Purchasing and Receiving	On time material delivery Cost effective raw materials Performance to specs	Receiving process Material ordering process Supplier management	Material cost per pound Avg. $ in inventory On time delivery %
Production	On time schedule completion Quality product Minimal waste	Preparation Assembly Packaging	Process cost per pound Rework / waste % % production to schedule
Shipping	On time shipments Accurate shipments Prompt order fulfillment	Order assembly Shipment scheduling Order labeling	On time % Order cycle time Shipping accuracy score

Key Support Processes

Key Support Process Area	Key Customer Requirements	Key Processes and Tools	Key Process Measure(s)
Accounting	Timely information Accurate information Minimize process costs	Month-end closing Receivables collection Billing and payroll	Monthly close cycle time # of days outstanding Process cost per pound
Human Resources	Quality employees Trained employees Value added benefits	Hiring process Training plan and delivery Benefits administration	Employee survey score Training index results Retention, absenteeism rates
Leadership	Effective strategies and plans Daily decision quality Process effectiveness	Performance reviews Planning sessions Workgroup meetings	Leadership Index Scorecard results Process cost per pound
Information Systems	Timely information Accurate information Reliable, friendly systems	Performance reports Intranet / internet PC applications	System uptime % # of user needs resolved Employee survey score
Quality Assurance	Timely feedback Quality training Accurate process monitoring	Defect tracking Complaint reduction process Quality Improvement teams	Defect rates # of customer complaints Employee survey score
Maintenance	Timely repairs Preventive maintenance Improvement projects	Downtime database, reports Scheduling process Project database	Equipment uptime % # of downtime incidents # of improvements made
Sanitation	Clean equipment and plant Food safety compliance Minimize waste streams	Master Cleaning Schedule Internal audits Recycling program	Daily pre-op scores Audit scores % waste recycled

Key Value Creation Processes - Park Place Lexus

Value Creation Process Area	Key Customer Requirements	Key Process Measures
New Car Sales (Prepare, engage, finalize, and sustain)	Sales consultant - courteous, knowledgeable Sales consultant - Respect time, honors commitments Courtesy client service	Survey score: Overall experience Survey score: Sales consultant approach Client concerns reported Avg. units sold / consultant Policy adjustments, days supply of cars Expenses, new cars sold
Pre-Owned Sales (Prepare, engage, finalize, and sustain)	Sales consultant - courteous, knowledgeable Sales consultant - Respect time, honors commitments Courtesy client service	Survey score: Overall experience Survey score: Sales consultant approach Client concerns reported Avg. units sold / consultant Policy adjustments, days supply of cars Expenses, pre-owned cars sold
Service (Make appointment, advise, service, repair, and follow up)	Quality of service - courteous, well explained Quality of service - informed of added work Quality of service - reviewed work performed Ease of doing business with - estimated time, greeted promptly Service communications - kept informed, documented needs Courtesy, client service	Survey score: Overall experience Survey score: Ready when promised Survey score: Fixed right first time Client concerns reported Service client re-checks Service revenue and retention % client paid revenue, expenses, WIP Technician productivity Reconditioning cycle time
Parts (Manage inventory, sell parts, receive and ship parts)	Courtesy, client service Sustained, cost effective inventory control Address client concerns	Survey Score: Parts availability Expenses, parts revenue Parts productivity, days of inventory, turns Client concerns reported
Finance and Insurance	Courtesy, client service Finance manager - discreet, efficient, recognizes needs	Survey score: Treats with respect Survey score: Overall handling Client concerns reported
Make Ready / Pick Up / Follow Up	Quality and on time make ready Courtesy, client service, contact Vehicle delivery personalized	Survey score: Delivery process Client concerns reported Policy adjustments
Vendor Management	Quality service / supplies Available when needed	# of vendor violations Cost savings $

Source: 2005 Park Place Lexus Baldrige Application Summary www.quality.nist.gov

On this page and the facing page, you will find examples of key process definition tables. I learned the value of using these tables as a Baldrige Examiner. Applicant organizations typically use a tool like this to define all of their key work processes. After defining the work processes themselves, the table is completed by adding the key customer requirements, and the measures for monitoring performance to those requirements, for each process.

The above example is from Park Place Lexus, a car dealership that received the award. Example processes and measures for a variety of healthcare processes are provided on the following two pages. One could argue that a complete and balanced set of measures has not been defined in all cases in these examples. While this maybe true in some cases, at least the effort has been made to begin linking processes, customer requirements, and measures.

Great Systems!
"Simple systems, great results!"

119

How Great are Your Key Health Care Process Measures?

Key Health Care Process Area	Process Measures	Le?	Tr?	S?	C?
Admitting	Wait time				
	Admission audit results				
	Occupancy				
	ER Door to MD cycle time				
	Registration accuracy				
	Registration cycle time				
	Denials due to no authorization				
	Patient satisfaction score				
	Physician satisfaction score				
Care Delivery	Infection rates				
	Medication errors				
	Mislabeled / unlabeled specimens				
	Patient falls				
	Unplanned returns				
	Cost per day				
	Length of stay				
	Mortality rates				
	# of potential avoidable days				
	JCAHO Core Measures				
Care Support	Turnaround time				
	Stockout rates				
	Nutrition assessment				
	Discrepancy rates				
	QA measures				
	Patient satisfaction score				
	Patient loyalty				
	Plan of care quality				
	Physician satisfaction score				
Discharge	Patient satisfaction score				
	Discharge instructions documented				
	Unplanned readmits				
	Average length of stay (ALOS)				
	Appropriate education provided				
	Gross days in AR				
	Monthly denials				
	% discharged but not final billed				

This table design allows you to evaluate the current status of each of your key measures:

Le - Performance Level – How well do current levels of performance for a given measure compare with defined goals and performance expectations?

Tr - Trends – Over the past 3-5 years, what type of trend has each measure been showing?

S – Segmentation – To what degree does segmented data for the measure exist?

C – Comparisons – How do performance levels compare with the selected benchmark?

How Great are Your Key Health Care Support Process Measures?

Key HC Support Process Area	Process Measures	Le?	Tr?	S?	C?
Human Resource Management	Employee turnover				
	Employee vacancy rate				
	Employee satisfaction with benefits				
	Training hours per FTE				
	Investment in employee development				
	Performance appraisal score				
	Employee satisfaction with leadership				
	Employee satisfaction score				
	Cost per hire				
Strategic Planning	Segmented market share				
	Occupancy rate				
	Community loyalty				
	# of physician partnerships				
	Priority objectives met				
	Public responsibility				
	Gallup performance survey				
	Employee satisfaction with plan awareness				
Financial Management	Days to final bill				
	Days cash on hand				
	Days in accounts receivable				
	Operating margin				
	Average age of PP&E				
	Inpatient / outpatient revenue				
	Days to monthly close				
	Patient satisfaction w/ billing				
	Charge process audit				
Supply Chain Management	Supplier report card scores				
	Inventory turns				
	Expense per patient discharge				
	Backorder rate				
	Returns to suppliers				
	Distributor fill rates				

This table lists the measures that are common to health care support processes. You may notice that there is a lot of similarity between the vital signs for health care support processes and support processes for other business sectors. As with the table on the facing page, this table is designed to allow one to evaluate current measure status.

This type of assessment tool is used in the Baldrige Performance Excellence process to help determine results effectiveness. High performance companies tend to do well in all four categories, for a majority of their key measures, across process types. Low performance companies struggle to even come up with a complete set of measures, let alone trend lines, goals, and benchmarks for those measures.

Great Systems!
"Simple systems, great results!"

The Ten Commandments of High Performance

I Design your leadership development system around a regular measurement process that comes from 'bottom up' reviews and is based on defined behavior and task expectations for all formal leaders.

II Redesign the jobs of your managers and supervisors to eliminate existing non-value added time usage and to include more time for skill practice, additional learning, coaching, and project work.

III Measure and improve the cost and effectiveness of all group events, such as training courses and meetings, that occur in your company.

IV Use formal decision making tools, such as a decision matrix, to prioritize and select improvement projects, instead of depending mostly on opinion.

V Use the majority of training time for skill practice and group interaction, as opposed to relying primarily on lecture as a means of teaching people how to do new things.

VI Link pay to performance for all employees, and install systems that pay people according to the degree of value they personally provide to the organization on a daily basis.

VII Use trend lines and control charts to understand and analyze all of your key processes, instead of using 'snapshot' tables of numbers as your primary process assessment tools.

VIII Define the owners, key requirements, and measures for all key processes, not just those that are performed in manufacturing or on the front lines.

IX Use process analysis and improvement to provide exceptional service to both your internal and external customers in a measurable manner that is linked to the key product / service requirements that they have helped you define.

X Improve the systems that you use to help ensure that new technologies are identified and implemented as soon as they become cost effective.

"The first step on the road to high performance begins with a choice."

Contact Information

E-mail: Kevin@greatsystems.com

Snail mail: 70460 Walker Road
Rainier, OR 97048

Phone: 206.226.8913

Website: www.greatsystems.com

TapRooT® Root Cause Analysis: www.taproot.com

About the Author

Kevin McManus is Chief Excellence Officer for Great Systems!, based in Rainer, OR and is a certified international trainer for the TapRooT® root cause analysis process. During his thirty plus years in the business world, he served as an Industrial Engineer, Training Manager, Production Manager, Plant Manager, and Director of Quality. Kevin's undergraduate (Industrial Engineering) and graduate (MBA) degrees blend together with his experience in six different manufacturing and service settings to help fuel and focus his efforts in organizational change and continuous systems improvement.

He continually seeks out opportunities to learn and to speak on topics related to organizational, team, and personal effectiveness. He has self-published several books and workbooks on systems improvement to help managers and supervisors develop a high performance workplace, including "You Can't Win Indy in an Edsel - How to Develop a High Performance Work Culture."

Kevin has served as an Examiner (1998), Senior Examiner (1999, 2000, 2001, 2002, 2003), and Alumni Examiner (2005, 2007, 2008, 2009, 2010, 2011, 2012, 2013, 2014, 2015) for the Malcolm Baldrige National Performance Excellence Award. For the past 15 years, he has written the monthly performance improvement column for *Industrial Engineer* magazine, and he has also served as Senior Vice President of Continuing Education for the Institute of Industrial Engineers.

As a member of the Association for Quality and Participation, he served as a chapter president, regional director, national Treasurer and Vice President, and national President of the Association. He is also a member of Toastmasters (ATM-S) and presents over 50 workshops and talks a year on the topics of performance improvement, root cause analysis, human error prevention, and process excellence.

Great Systems!
"Simple systems, great results!"

Vital Signs, Scorecards, and Goals

www.ingramcontent.com/pod-product-compliance
Lightning Source LLC
Chambersburg PA
CBHW041454210326
41599CB00005B/247